A Boy on the
LAST BOAT

Published by Brolga Publishing Pty Ltd
ABN 46 063 962 443
PO Box 12544
A'Beckett St
Melbourne, VIC, 8006
Australia

email: markzocchi@brolgapublishing.com.au

National Library of Australia
Cataloguing-in-Publication data
        Lochtenberg, Ben, author.
        A Boy On the last Boat / A Journey Around the World
        ISBN: 9781925367416 (paperback)
        Subjects: Family--Australia--Biography--World War,
        1939-1945--History-Indonesia-- Japanese occupation--
        Personal narratives.
        Dewey Number: 620.0092

Printed in Australia
Cover design by   Chameleon Design
Typesetting by   Elly Cridland

BE PUBLISHED

Publish through a successful publisher. National distribution, Macmillan & International distribution to the United Kingdom, North America. Sales Representation to South East Asia
Email: markzocchi@brolgapublishing.com.au

A Boy on the
LAST BOAT

A Journey Around the World

BEN LOCHTENBERG

For Margaret and our children,
Jan, Anna, Mark, Michael, Benedict, Maggie and Lucy,
and in memory of my Mother and Father.

Acknowledgements

When I retired in 1993 I set myself the objective of writing a family history. I was prompted to do this by my children and my dear wife Margaret.

Since then it has become an intermittent and challenging task, and has led me to reflect repeatedly on the good fortune I have experienced in countless ways throughout my life.

Professor Elaine Barry, a cousin of my wife Margaret, was the first to review and provide encouraging comment on this memoir. Since then Fiona Maloney and my daughters Margaret Mary and Lucy, have each provided invaluable input and support.

I am indebted to Lynne and Wayne Robinson and Terry Herbert who introduced me to Mark Zocchi of Brolga Publishing, where Tara Wylie and Elly Cridland have provided essential and much appreciated editing and support. I am grateful to them all.

Preface

I didn't know when I was ten, that I would never see my father again.

While I only had some early years with my father, I hope I have carried out his last wish to me:

"That Daddy's dearest and only son will always remember his Dad … and that Ben grows up to be honest and strong, is the only wish of his loving father".

My life has been very different to those of my parents and particularly my father.

It has puzzled me why my father, apart from some early happy years of marriage, suffered so much before he died in 1945 at the age of 42 when building a railway in Sumatra, Indonesia as a Japanese prisoner of war. After my father's death, my mother suffered forty years of loneliness and depression, before dying at the age of 83 in 1987. Both my parents typify the countless millions disrupted and traumatised by the 1939-1945 war. This suffering is additional to the estimated 60 to 70 million who lost their lives then. In stark contrast, I escaped the war and more recent conflicts, unscathed to lead a full and rewarding life. God and fate work in mystifying and unexpected ways.

Since my retirement, I have had the chance to reflect on my life journey and more importantly those of my parents, and like many have become increasingly nomadic, crossing borders cultures and customs. My early aim was to write primarily about my father, whom I never knew well. But when I discovered that my mother's great-great-grandmother was Chinese I began writing also about my maternal grandmother, Anna Rosa's, family. I began to understand then my mother's family background and why I was born in Singapore.

More recently, I have written also about my wife Margaret and our lives, adding personal reflections such as my religious beliefs to the interwoven tales of my family. My refugee origin suggested a title for this work which relates more to my and my mother's background rather than my father's, whose family historical details are very limited.

Writing memoirs and family histories has become popular in recent years. I have reflected on the reason for this. The novelist George Orwell suggested four motives for such writings:

"First is sheer egoism, next aesthetic enthusiasm, third historical impulse or the desire to see things as they are, and lastly political purpose and the urge to persuade".

Simon Schama the British historian has added:

"A fight against loss, an instinct for replay, a resistance to the attrition of memory."

This last motive resonates with my own feelings as to why I have attempted to write about my family history despite many omissions and errors.

Hagedorn &
Von Hartwig
Family Tree

Friedrich Carl R P Von Hartwig
B: 28 Mar 1819 - Emden, Germany
M: 1854 - East Java, Indonesia
D: 7 Oct 1899 - Singapore

Marianne Emilie E Von Hartwig
B: 17 Mar 1849 - Sumatra
M: 6 Apr 1868 - Singapore
D: 25 Sep 1905 - Singapore

Tja Kin Nja
B: 1825 - Indonesia
M: 1854 - East Java, Indonesia
D: 15 Mar 1894 - Singapore

Friedrich "Egmont" Hagedorn
B: 1815
M: 1 Jun 1842 - Hamburg, Germany
D: 1890

Johann Emil "Egmont" Hagedorn
B: 2 May 1843 - Hamburg
M: 6 Apr 1868 - Singapore
D: 14 Aug 1882 - Singapore

Christian Rosalie "Rosa" Simon
B: 3 Sep 1816 - Hamburg, Germany
M: 1 Jun 1842 - Hamburg, Germany
D: 13 Mar 1852 - Hamburg, Germany

Anna Rosa Angelica "Baby" Hagedorn
B: 31 Jul 1881 - Singapore
M: 18 Feb 1897 - The Good Shepherd, Singapore
D: 9 Sep 1966 - Australia

Hendrick Jan Coenraad Heytman
B: 11 Sep 1868 - Utrecht, Holland
M: 18 Feb 1897 - The Good Shepherd, Singapore
D: 22 Dec 1934 - Singapore

William Hendrick Heytman
B: Holland
M: -
D: -

Continued on next page

Catharina Helena Schook/Shoek
B: Holland
M: -
D: -

Jan Bernard
B: 9 Jan 1957 - Liverpool

Anna Catherine
B: 25 Apr 1958 - Melbourne

Mark Hamish
B: 10 Sep 1960 - Dumbarton

Michael Dermot
B: 12 May 1962 - Melbourne

Benedict John
B: 12 Nov 1963 - Melbourne

Margaret Mary
B: 2 May 1965 - Melbourne

Kate Emma Lucy
B: 3 Apr 1973 - Melbourne

Margaret Mary Lynch
B: 4 Sep 1931 - Brisbane
M: 16 Jun 1956 - London

Bernard Hendrik Lochtenberg
B: 10 Mar 1931 - Singapore
M: 16 Jun 1956 - London

Anna Heytman
B: 10 Aug 1903 - Singapore
M: 25 Jan 1929 - The Good Shepherd, Singapore
D: 4 Jun 1987 - Melbourne Australia

Jan Marie Lochtenberg
B: 25 Nov 1902 - Amsterdam, Holland
M: 25 Jan 1929 - Singapore
D: 6 May 1945 – Pekan Baroe, Sumatra

CONTENTS

1

Mum's Family

My early childhood was spent in Singapore, where I was born in 1931, and I then moved to Java at the age of 2 in 1933.

I was not aware until I looked into my family history, that my Mother had a Chinese forebear in the mid-19th century. The 1930s was a period when colonial empires of the British and the Dutch were coming to an end. War with Japan ended a colonial era for these far-eastern islands which were never to be the same again. British and particularly Dutch attempts to reclaim their colonies after the Japanese military occupation were doomed to failure. The Allied defeat of the Japanese in 1945 released pent-up nationalism in Malaysia and Indonesia. Pre-war affluent, indulgent and often repressive colonial ways did not survive the newly established Southeast Asian nations of Singapore, Malaysia and Indonesia.

The region was changed forever.

Singapore, once a critically important colony in the British Empire, is strategically located on the shipping route between India and China. The city's population is primarily Chinese.

In colonial times, its streets were choked not with cars but with carts, rickshaws and pedestrians scurrying through the crowded city, permeated with the distinctive sounds and pungent, spicy cooking smells of the Orient.

Singapore is only 640 square kilometres in area, with no natural resources has a mixed population today of less than two million mainly ethnic Chinese. The island, sandwiched between Malaysia and Indonesia, was founded by Sir Stamford Raffles who purchased it from the Sultan of Johore.

With very little authority but a great deal of colonial bravado, Raffles held a ceremony on Singapore Island on 6th February 1819 to recognise Tunku Hussein as the rightful Sultan of Johore. His Highness the Sultan later signed a second treaty which allowed Raffles to build a British settlement on Singapore in return for payments of $5000 and $3000 a year respectively to the Sultan and the Temenggong, his chief official.

The British flag was hoisted and gunshots rang out in a simple ceremony to mark the foundation of Singapore which then became a British colony. Raffles wrote to his employer, "The East India Company" (EIC), in London, "You take my word for it, this is by far the most important station in the East; and as far as naval superiority and commercial interests are concerned, of much higher value."

A territorial dispute with the Dutch was resolved in London five years later in March 1824 when The British acquired Malacca, Penang and Singapore, while the Dutch were given undisputed control of Java and Sumatra. In 1819 the island was occupied sparsely by no more than 1000 fishermen and their families. As a result of no port duties, 139 square rigged ships and 1434 native vessels called into Singapore to trade. By the time of the first census held in 1824 the population had reached 10,683, and by 1911 totalled 311,303.[1]

A Sumatran Prince had earlier called the settlement, known locally as Temasek (sea town), as Singapura or "Lion City". In 1826 the EIC amalgamated Singapore, Penang and Melaka into the Straits Settlements which remained under EIC control until 1867 when it became a British colony, and a British naval base until 1942. Singapore aspired to nationhood after the Second World War. At first it was part of the Federation of Malaysia, and it became an independent state and then a nation in August 1965.

To this day it remains a vital trading centre strategically located on the sea route between China and India, and most ships still have to pass Singapore. The sea roads outside Keppel Harbour where ships wait their turn to come to port or be unloaded have always been among the most congested in the East. Its remarkable growth is attributed to its prime location and because it was a free port, whereas the Dutch in Batavia and the Spanish in Manila levied tariffs and charges on imports, as did local rulers in smaller ports. Singapore became a critically important commercial and naval link in Britain's empire.

This growing centre of trade attracted Chinese merchants and immigrant labour from China, and the tin mining industry which developed in the Malay States was created by Chinese entrepreneurs who were granted concessions

---

1 'The Battle for Singapore', Peter Thompson. Portrait Books, 2005. p 319-322

by Malay Rulers. Colonial life in the 19th and early 20th century is described well in the short stories by the writer Somerset Maughan.

In the quiet outlying eastern suburb of Singapore named Katong, beyond the then very small city airport, stood the two storied colonial rambling home of my grandparents, the Heytmans, with whom my newly married parents lived initially. I was born in Singapore's maternity hospital historically named "Sepoy Lines", the name referring to the Indian soldiers garrisoned in the Colony. My childhood recollections are mainly of my grandparents and their home set well back from Meyer road. An early memory is of my grandmother, Anna Rosa Heytman (1881-1966), who was a Hagedorn before marrying my Dutch grandfather, Hendrik Heytman who was born in 1868.

Anna Rosa was a formidable, competent, and to me, a wonderful and very loving person. Although supported by many servants, she almost single-handedly raised her large family of 7 daughters and 4 sons. Her third child, Elsie, died when 14 months old, and fourth child, Erick, died after 7 months, so these two were just names to me among my many aunts, uncles and cousins in Singapore.

Anna Rosa, although born in Singapore, descended from two German families from Hamburg named Godeffroy and von Hartwig. The former were originally Huguenots who escaped religious persecution in France when the Edict of Nantes was revoked in 1685. This traumatic event resulted in the migration that year of some 200,000 to 300,000 French Huguenots who fled to other parts of Europe. The Huguenots were French Protestants and members of the church established in 1550 by John Calvin. The origin of the name is unknown, but possibly "Huis Genooten", or "house fellows" to describe students gathered in each other's houses to study the Bible secretly in the Flemish border of France. Huguenots became known for open criticism of the Roman Catholic Church, which led to religious wars and their persecution in France during the 16th and 17th centuries. At least 200,000 French Huguenots fled to countries such as Switzerland, Germany and England, where they could enjoy religious freedom.

The Godeffroy family settled in Hamburg and established a trading and shipping business. Today there is an outlying street named Godeffroy near the summer houses built by family members in the late 18th century.

The Godeffroy family tree shows Anna Rosa's French grandmother Rosalie Simon (1816 - 1852) who was married to Friedrich Egmont Hagedorn (1815 - 1890). The Godeffroys once they were established in Germany became successful and wealthy. I was told about a visit Anna Rosa made prior to the 1st World War in 1914 to her family in Hamburg. Family dinners were served on gold plate by uniformed servants. Anna Rosa and her husband Hendrik then also went to Utrecht in Holland to see my grandfather Hendrik's family.

My grandmother Anna Rosa was the 10th and youngest child of Johann Emil "Egmont" Hagedorn (1843-1882) who was born in Hamburg. On 4th May 1865, two days after his 22nd birthday, Egmont Hagedorn left Europe for Singapore where he found employment with the trading firm Zapp & Baur on Collyer Quay.

After several years he was made a partner in the firm. The family told me Egmont became the German Consul in Singapore, and he probably held this position part-time. Egmont married my great grandmother Marianne von Hartwig (1849 – 1905) on 6th April 1868 at Singapore's Presbyterian Church.

This 19-year-old bride, Marianne, was born on the 17th March 1849 in Pangkal Pinang-Muntok on Bangka Island off the East coast of Sumatra.

Marianne was baptised in Muntok on 16th October 1941 with the names of Maria Anna Emilia Ernestina Emma. She had mixed parentage with a German father Friedrich Carl von Hartwig (1819 – 1894) and his "nyonya" or concubine Tja Kin Nja. Tja was born in Palembang Sumatra in 1825, the daughter of a Chinese "Tin Lord" secret-society chief involved in tin mining on Bangka Island.

The Dutch brought workers from China to Bangka Island in the 18th Century, in order to develop the island's tin mines. Bangka was ceded to Britain by the Sultan of Palembangin 1812, but in 1814 was exchanged with the Dutch for Cochin in India.

The island was occupied by the Japanese from 1942 to 1945, and became part of independent Indonesia in 1949.

The island together with nearby Belitung was formerly part of South Sumatra, but in 2000 the two islands became the new Province of Bangka-Belitung.

Bangka is famous for the massacre in WWII of Australian nurses by the Japanese army, as recorded by Sister Vivian

Bullwinkel[2] and is reportedly the setting for the book 'Lord Jim' by Joseph Conrad.

Bangka has also been home since the 1960's for a number of communist Indonesians under house arrest not permitted to leave the island.

The earliest known use of tin was in the Bronze Age, and there is linguistic evidence of indo-Chinese tin miners in Malaysia, centuries before Christ.

From the 5th to 9th century Indian miners produced tin used for Hindu images. In recent times, tin has been used in Europe for pewter, and today for canning and in motor vehicles. From the 18th century Chinese had a tin mining monopoly in the South East region, attracting immigrants from districts around Canton, who were known as Si Yap (Ssu Yi) or "Four Towns".

The work was hard but profitable. Even in 1912, 80% of the 750 Malaysian tin mines were in Chinese hands and in 1941 they owned one-third of the mines around Ipoh in Malaysia.

Friedrich and Tja had five children before marrying in Surabaya, Java on 23 June 1854. The couple married to avoid ostracism and be accepted when they moved to Singapore.

Marianne's father, Friedrich, had travelled from Hamburg to Amsterdam in 1838, at the age of 19, to join as a soldier in the "German Division" of the Dutch army; it was common at that time for the Dutch army to recruit foreign mercenaries.

---

2 'The Battle of Singapore' Peter Thompson. p 324

Friedrich was promoted to corporal before being shipped, in 1839, to Batavia in the East Indies.

The voyage then was challenging, taking 115 days. Sea travel in the early 19th century was arduous and non-military passengers provided their own bedding, washbasin, ewer and chamber-pot, cutlery and any furniture such as desk or chairs to be used in their future home. There are few records of Friedrich's army movements after 1839, except for the recorded births of his five children who included Marianne, the eldest.

He was promoted to sergeant-major in 1841, moving that year to Surabaya which was then the military headquarters for East Java.

In 1856 he resigned from the army after his marriage to Tja Kin Nja. The family with their five children moved to Singapore in 1858, where Friedrich became a ship chandler, an essential and important role in any port.

The business supplied water and provisions to ships in Singapore harbour. By 1860 the business was widely known as von Hartwig and Co.[3] The population of Singapore in 1860 was 81,734, and of that year's 11,000 immigrants, 7700 arrived by junk and 3200 by square rigged ships (ibid), so that many of the town's ship chandlers were also sail makers.

Friederich as a prominent local businessman would have cut a fine figure in the Colony.

"He would be seen in the morning at the harbour docks

---

3 'One Hundred Years of Singapore' Roland St John Braddell, Gilbert
    E. Brooke and Walter Makepeace.

    (ibid) - citing the same reference as the prior footnote source.

in a pair of white calico trousers and ordinary shirt, the ends of which instead of being tucked in hung outside. A pith hat and stout stick completed the picture. Between three and four in the afternoon he would head for town. If the day was fine he would then put on the shiniest of Calcutta-made patent leather shoes, the whitest of duck trousers, no waistcoat but a spotless white cotton shirt with turned down collar and black silk bow and straight-cut coat, with a black silk hat covering his head ready for the evening." (ibid)

The eldest daughter of Friedrich and Tja Kin Nja, was thus my great grandmother Marianne von Hartwig who married Egmont Hagedorn in Singapore at the age of 19 on 16th April 1868. Egmont continued to work in Singapore as a merchant until his death in 1882 following a long battle with heart illness.

Marianne following his death remained a widow for 23 years bringing up eight of her ten children aged 1 to 12.

The two eldest boys were educated in Hamburg having been taken there earlier by their father. The youngest child, aged 1, when Egmont died, was my grandmother Anna Rosa who therefor never knew her father. Marianne spoke German, as well as Chinese and Malay and her grandchildren referred to her as "Oma".

The two eldest sons were sent to Germany and were never able to establish a relationship with their mother.

Later in Marianne's estate they were cut off with 5 pounds each, perhaps because they benefited by receiving a European education. But there could also have been a family rift, due to their mother being half Chinese.

Marianne died on 25th September 1905 in Singapore where she is buried. She would have been lonely, and ostracised, after her husband's death. Dinner invitations and entry to Singapore Clubs would have ended abruptly and social relationships cut off or become strained.

It is likely that former friends would no longer acknowledge her publically and she is likely to have been miserable in the class-conscious Singapore society.

Myrna Blake, a descendant of Marianne's sister, Caroline Asmus nee von Hartwig and author of "Singapore Eurasians", wrote in a letter in September 1993 about the social aspects of being Eurasian at the time:

The "European" and "Eurasian" difference reflects the process of social stratification – the strata becoming more clearly defined as the "mixed" community became larger and threatening to the "whites" – at least in the job market, so that the white community needed to draw boundaries. Eurasians, who could "pass" as white, often attempted to do so. It was painful to be mixed. Not only was any Asian background hidden but in many cases, it was actually denied.

My understanding of these distinctions made me hesitate about the possibility of my mother being at a Hagedorn party (in the late 1920's). Hagedorns would have been "upper ten" – white Eurasians.

I suspect that my mother's family might not have been completely accepted - though they may have been aspiring to. Acceptance of my mother would have hinged on her marriage to my father, whose acceptability was linked to his professional status. It is my hunch that girls if they were pretty and educated, contributed to the upward social mobility of families. Beautiful Eurasian women were brought up to be social butterflies – decorative, charming, and socially polished.

So late in my life I learned that Marianne, the mother of my grandma Anna Rosa, was half Chinese and hence Eurasian. I discovered that not only am I $\frac{1}{16}$ Chinese but also $\frac{1}{16}$ French, the latter through Anna Rosa's father "Egmont" Hagedorn being a descendant from the Godeffroy family.

I was strangely pleased to learn of this mixed family background and it made sense of my Singapore birth. Needless to say, the information was greeted with surprise by Margaret and our children!

My Singapore background going back several generations has made me think more about the social pressures experienced by my great grandmother, grandmother and mother living in a colonial community of mixed races. As a major shipping and trading centre Singapore included races from all over the world, with Europeans interspersed with a wide range of Asians. Although these were dominantly Chinese, they also included Indians, Japanese and Filipinos with many different cultures and religions.

Colonial Europeans looked down on Asians not recognising the latter's culture and history despite these predating those of Europe.

An inevitable outcome of the interaction between races was that some Europeans married Asians and their children were labelled "half-caste" and discriminated against. I became aware that this also affected my family as my mother's brothers Willy and Bertie had married Asian women named Muriel and Pearline respectively, although this was never shared or discussed with me. Mum's third brother, Harold, married an English girl named Elsie.

I do not know how she came to be in Singapore, but I recall uncharitable family comments that Harold had married "a London barmaid", another indication of their ingrained prejudices.

The concern of colonials not to be recognised as being of mixed race was reflected in the tendency of my mother's family to embellish their background, and stories of family past greatness abounded. This was reinforced by my mother's family not only having been born but also educated in Singapore. They felt at a disadvantage to European arrivals which followed the colonial practice of sending children to Europe for their education.

This custom also minimised children becoming overindulged by servants and hopefully would inculcate appropriate values and manners. It is therefore not surprising that I know nothing of any schools in Singapore attended by my mother and her siblings, and they never spoke of this.

Mum and her five sisters married Europeans except for Eileen who married an Australian who worked on a tin operation in Malaya, and Kitty, the eldest sister who married an accountant from South Africa. Nan married an English engineer employed at the city's power station: Alice, a Channel Islander, working in Singapore for Cadbury's Chocolate, and Dorothy married a Swiss whom she met after the war. Mum of course married my father, a Dutchman. It is difficult to appreciate these colonial race issues in today's multicultural Australia, where Mandarin has replaced Italian and also Greek as the most common foreign language spoken today, and Asia has displaced Europe as the main source of our immigrants.

It was in Singapore that my grandmother, Anna Rosa, met my Dutch grandfather, Hendrik Heytman. Anna was only 16 when Hendrik married her on the 18th February 1897 in the Cathedral of the Good Shepherd. The marriage was officiated by the Apostolic Missionary Fr DeLouette as the Catholic Church in Singapore was staffed at that time by an order of French priests from Siam, now Thailand. It was not unusual then for girls to marry at such an early age, but one can wonder how my 29 year old grandfather met this young colonial schoolgirl. The marriage was witnessed by "M. Hagedorn", Anna Rosa's mother Marianne, and the couple set up house in Paterson Street Tanglin.

Grandfather Hendrik Jan Coenraad Heytman 1868 - 1934 (original spelling "Heijtman"?), was born in Utrecht and lived in the Bisa suburb at Langenieuwe Weg 74. His parents Willem Hendrick Heytman and Catharina Helena Schook (or Shoek?) had married on the 9th November 1865. Hendrik had two brothers, one named Rijk who I was told was no less than an Admiral in the Dutch navy! Perhaps yet another example of my family's "Darshan", which is the wonderful Indian expression of the beneficial glow one derives from being in the presence of, or associated with, an important person. Hendrik's other brother Kees worked a quinine estate in Java, whom I will refer to later. I was also told that Hendrik's grandfather was a Professor of Mathematics at Leiden University. Certainly Leiden was a renowned centre of mathematics and astronomy in the 19th and earlier centuries, and I felt some irrational and possibly groundless pleasure from thinking that this forebear could be the source of my aptitude in mathematics!

Grandfather Hendrik left Holland on a sailing ship for Dili in Timor aged about 24 or 25. He moved later to Singapore where he met and married 16 year old Anna Rosa in 1897. As a child I was told that grandfather Hendrik was the Dutch Consul in Singapore, but in later years I learned that he was an immigration official in the Dutch Consulate, having worked earlier in the Post Office.

What is now clear is that the family's later prosperity was based primarily on Anna Rosa, who inherited her wealth from her German uncle Godeffroy, who was childless and left his estate to his nephews and nieces including Anna Rosa.

2

The Godeffroys

The Godeffroys were a well to do French Huguenot family from La Rochelle.

Following the 1685 religious exodus from France, the earliest record of a Godeffroy in Germany is of Cesar III (1703 - 1758) a wine merchant who settled initially in Berlin moving later to Hamburg, where his son Jean Cesar IV (1742 - 1818) purchased a property, now called "Deer Park", on Elbchausee. In 1766, Jean Cesar's son, Johann Cesar V, established the Godeffroy family trading business J.C.Godeffroy & Sohne. (Das Haus an der Elbchaussee" Gabrielle Hoffman 1999).

Hamburg by then had become the wealthiest city in Europe having been granted duty free trade along the lower Elbe by Emperor Frederick Barbarossa in 1189. The Godeffroy business traded initially with Spain, and Central and South American ports such as Havana, where Cesar VI (1813 - 1885) and his brother Adolphe, established a branch in 1837.

As narrated by their friend Alexander Friedrick

Kleinwort who later founded the Kleinwort Benson Bank:

"The business and the private life of the Godeffroy gentlemen in Havana is wild, as there is plenty to amuse and distract them with opera house, balls, carnivals, cockpits and bullfights, as well as innumerable concerts and theatrical performances" [4]

The Godeffroys became ship owners, as well as merchants, and founded in Hamburg the famous Hamburg-Amerika shipping line and later the Museum Godeffroy, which existed from 1861 to 1885 and was founded by Johann Cesar 6th Godeffroy, whose ship captains brought back zoological, botanical and ethnographic material from the Pacific. A rare Samoan butterfly is still named "Papilio godeffroyi" commonly known as Godeffroy's Swallowtail. The Museum was located in the Kontorhausen (counting house building) of the Company's office in Hamburg. Before his death in 1885, Godeffroy sold the Museum collection to museums in Leipzig, Hamburg, Berlin, Leiden, Oxford and Dundee.

Papilio godeffroyi butterfly
(Godeffroy's Swallowtail)

---

4 'The History of two Families in Banking' Kleinwort Benson
   Johanne Wake OUP 1997, p 65 & 70

The museum sponsored scientific research in the South Pacific as an offshoot of the Godeffroy trading activity based in Apia, Samoa in the 1850s. There is a monument, now neglected and hidden by foliage, in front of the Casino Hotel in Apia once the Pacific headquarters of the Company. It bears the German inscription:

"Jon Cesar Godeffroy 1813 - 1885. Here was founded the Jon Cesar Godeffroy und Sohn, Hamburg, in the year 1885, their first branch in the South Seas".[5]

The Godeffroy ships traded all over the world by 1856, and began the first regular service to Australia. They brought German immigrants from Hamburg, landing them in Moreton Bay Queensland. The ships would then sail to Samoa and other Godeffroy Pacific island trading posts. The ships would load coconut products such as copra and coconut oil and 'mother of pearl' shell, before returning to Europe. Coconut is far and away the most important nut crop in the world. Its native origin was in the islands of Indonesia, yet coconuts were found by the first Europeans when they arrived in the Caribbean and on the Pacific Coast of Central America. There are now about 3.5 million hectares of coconut plantations in the Philippines, India, Indonesia, Sri Lanka and the Caribbean. Coconuts grow in the Tropics, yet can withstand slight frost.

Besides providing nutritious meat and coconut milk, oil extracted from the dried meat has been used for centuries for cooking and frying as well as in the manufacture of soaps, cosmetics and lubricants. After extracting the oil, dried copra cake can be ground to a meal high in protein,

---

5 'Queen Emma', Pacific Publications, Sydney 1965. p 26

used for cattle and chicken feed while the trunk provides roof beams and the fibres of the husk, known as coir, is used to make ropes.[6]

Coconut products have been traded extensively as was done by the Godeffroy Company in the 19th century. Coconut oil was shipped to Europe in lengths of bamboo each holding 3 gallons, used to light street lamps in London and Oslo. The German Godeffroy business in the Pacific located in Samoa and Eastern New Guinea became German colonies in 1900.

These were annexed subsequently by the Allies, in 1918, after the defeat of Germany in World War One. German names in the Pacific today such as "The Bismarck Archipelago" are a reminder of this early trading history.

The J.C. Godeffroy & Sohne Company's fortunes survived the Hamburg bank crash of 1857 but in 1879 the Company was forced into bankruptcy as a result of investing in Russian paper, and Westphalian mining.

The remnants of the Godeffroy business empire, which at its peak included 27 ships and associated world trading operations, would still have represented a considerable fortune. A fraction of the surviving Godeffroy estate was left to my grandmother, Anna Rosa, in the early 1930s from an uncle in Germany.

Another branch of the Godeffroys not connected to the Heytman/Hagedorn family, had married into the Bülow family, which later included Bernhard von Bülow who became Chancellor of the German Empire, and General Adolph von Bülow who served in the First World War.

---

6 '1421 – The year China discovered the world' by Gavin Menzies. p 399

I only mention these because my mother and her family often regaled me in my childhood with misplaced pride of the von Bulow connection.

A recent conjunction related to the Godeffroys, or as Margaret and I believe to be "two and not six degrees of separation", concerns a dinner in 2003 we had at "Buca Di Sant Antionio" in Lucca Italy, a renowned restaurant established in 1782. At the time, Margaret was enrolled in an Italian language class in Lucca.

When we arrived at the restaurant, we were directed to the basement and I complained in rather a loud voice that the locals were seated upstairs and we "Turisti" were placed downstairs! We were sitting next to a German couple and during the meal we began to converse. It turned out that our dining companions, the Dieter Wittwers, were from Hamburg, and I explained that my grandmother also originated there and being a Hagedorn, descended from the Godeffroy family. Mr Wittwer was startled saying he was then in the middle of reading a book about the Godeffroys which he found fascinating! He promised to see if there was an English edition. Unfortunately there is not, but he did send us the Godeffroy family tree.

The book details the history of the Godeffroy family, and the title relates to the Godeffroy summer house on the Elbe. The encounter prompted me to buy the book and I very much regret my lack of proficiency in German.

Margaret and I were able to visit Hamburg in January 2005. We stayed at the Vierjahreszeiten Hotel where I had stayed previously when on Imperial Chemical Industries (ICI) business in 1960. The hotel is centrally located on the city's inner harbour.

We took a taxi to the Godeffroy summer home at 499 Elbe Chaussee, a beautiful avenue south of the city which runs along the Elbe River and has always been much sought after by Hamburg's wealthy families. En route we passed "das Weisse Haus", now a hotel. I had been confused in my Godeffroy internet research, having mistakenly assumed this had been the family summer home. The hotel was only reopened in 2001 after having previously been the Park Hotel in the 1850's. This was yet another of my fruitless blind alleys, which is hardly surprising when following up numerous internet leads, which nevertheless provided me with much Godeffroy information.

Margaret and I struck gold at number 499 Elbchaussee. The front door was opened by a Mrs Christianne Meyer-Rogge who runs a ballet school on the ground floor of this former Godeffroy summer home. She was starting a class and there were several chattering young girls in the entrance to the house. As she was occupied, she called her husband who invited us to their upstairs private living quarters for tea. He proceeded to talk rapidly in his attempt to be helpful. The house turned out to be the summer residence of Cesar VI that had lived from 1813 to 1885. The property had previously included a farm and three adjoining estates on the Elbe River outside Hamburg, and was purchased in 1786 for 33,000 Reichstaller by Cesar 4th (1742 - 1818). On one side of the front drive there is a thatch covered restaurant called the Witt Hus (499a). This was the original 1786 farmhouse converted by Godeffroy to the "Kavaliershaus" to accommodate guests of the main house.

In 1889 the extensive gardens of the house became a municipal park known as the "Hirschpark" or" Deer Park", with an existing double row of Linden trees dating back to Cesar IV, and high banks of rhododendrons which must be a picture in spring.

We learned that the ballet school had been founded in 1927 by Christianne's mother Lola Rogge, a ballerina from Russia. The house is now rented by Peter and Christianne from the municipality, and a plaque in the entrance portico records the Godeffroy origin. The municipal ownership no doubt explains the rather run down look of the property, but it was good to see the house being used as a ballet school. Peter Meyer-Rogge, although garrulous, was very helpful and explained that there was another Godeffroy summer house built by Cesar's younger brother Peter at 547 Elbchaussee. Peter, was in fact, the direct forbear of my grandmother Anna Rosa, with three intervening generations of Emily Godeffroy, Rosalie Simon, and Egmont Hagedorn. Myer Rogge explained that both Godeffroy houses had been designed by the Royal Danish architect, Hansen. He showed us a book that detailed the Palladian style of the architect. (Royal Masterbuilder "Christian Frederik Hansen in Hamburg, Altona und der Elbvoroen", ein Danisher Architek des Keasismus, 2000 Altonaer Museum im Hamburg).

Hansen (1756 - 1845) designed and built 22 houses along the Elbe for many prominent Hamburg families including the Thornton family from England.

This latter house still exists with stables at 215 and 228 Elbe High Road, and it is likely that Peter Godeffroy's wife, Catherina Thornton, was a member of this family who lived nearby. We finally took leave of our helpful host and took a short walk through the gardens along broken muddy paths as it was winter, stopping at the Withus restaurant for a delicious quiche lunch. We bought some postcards and a magazine describing the Godeffroy house and neighbourhood. We then ordered a taxi to find Peter Godeffroy's house at number 547. This was located off Godefroy Avenue and is an extremely well maintained mansion, set in large manicured lawns. I rang the front door bell tentatively. Having received no response, I tried again and after a long pause heard bolts being drawn on the large double doors and was faced by an irritated middle-aged man. I explained who we were and our Godeffroy family connection and asked if we could take a picture of the house, hoping of course to be invited inside. After a long pause, he said in German, "Alright just one picture" and then slammed the door shut! We were very disappointed with his response and to meet such a short-tempered and inhospitable person. We learned later that he is a member of the Essberger von Rantzau family.

The Essberger von Rantzau family are connected with the failed plot to kill Hitler on 20th July 1944. The plot involved Count von Stauffenberg who placed a briefcase containing a bomb under a map table in the briefing room of the "Wolf's Lair", Hitler's headquarters in East Prussia. The conspiracy leaders included Adam von Trott zu Solz (a pre-war German Rhodes Scholar) and his Foreign Office colleague Josias von Rantzau, who alone escaped Hitler's wrath.

After the war von Rantzau was deported to the USSR and is said to have died in Moscow's Lubyanka prison.[7] We beat a retreat and returned to the city by taxi with a brief stop at "Das Weisse Haus" hotel, and were not successful in locating the Godeffroy Museum as it was closed in 1885.

We learned that the homes of Cesar (no 499) and Peter (no 547) were used at the end of the war following the surrender of Hamburg by General Major Wolz to General Spurling of the British 7th Tank Division, on the 3rd May 1945. British officers took up residence in No 547 which was used as a mess room. Cesar's house, at No 499, was used as a school building for children of the occupying armed forces.

The park and associated properties were returned by the British to the Hamburg authorities only in 1957! We returned to our Vier Jahreszeiten hotel to reflect on the day's events. All in all, the day's search had been successful, and we reflected on our good fortune that the two Godeffroy summer houses were still in use. Being holiday retreats well outside the city centre, they escaped the Allied fire bombing raid in May 1943, which doubtless destroyed the principal residences of brothers Cesar, and Peter.

Although cities like Warsaw and Rotterdam had been bombed in the opening stages of the war, both Germany and Britain were reluctant to start massive bombing of civilian targets. Even the Battle of Britain was at first essentially a series of dogfights for supremacy in the air.

But in May 1940, the British Cabinet agreed to the all-

7 'The Berlin Diaries of Marie Vassiltchikov', 1985 Chatto and Windus, Folio Society 1991

out bombing of civilian targets in Germany. On the night of 24 August 1940 German bombers dropped some bombs on London by mistake. The following night, the RAF retaliated with a raid by 80 bombers on Berlin.

Incensed, Hitler thereupon ordered the Luftwaffe to cease targeting British harbours, industry and RAF ground installations, and concentrate instead on London. This decision was to cost Hitler the "Battle of Britain", for just when British air defences were at their weakest and German victory in the air in sight, the RAF was able to rebuild its strength. But from then on, the indiscriminate bombing of civilian populations became official policy on all fronts of the war.

"Operation Gomorrah" launched on Hamburg on 27th July 1943 and conducted jointly by the Royal Air Force Bomber Command at night and the US 8th Air Force by day, was the heaviest and most destructive assault in the history of aerial warfare. For the first time phosphorous bombs were used on such a scale so as to create "fire-storms" and hurricane-like winds which destroyed and killed more than the bombs themselves. Hot air soared thousands of feet into the sky, creating a vacuum at ground level that was filled by winds gusting at 150 mph. Buildings were destroyed and people were hurled through the air. Some were burned in the street or in their homes by the sheer intensity of the heat.

Other victims were stuck in the roadways as asphalt turned to boiling liquid. Thousands were asphyxiated by lack of oxygen or died of smoke inhalation having sought shelter in cellars. For the first time the Allies used metallic strips dropped in bundles to confuse enemy radar and flak.

The raids of Hamburg left 45,000 dead (compared with the 40,000 killed by the atomic bombing of Nagasaki) and over a million civilians were made homeless. It reduced half the city to rubble and cut all services so that the population had to be evacuated. The destruction involved 250 square kilometres of the most densely built-up area of the city. Over ten days Allied aircraft dropped 9000 tonnes of explosives and incendiaries. A total of 3095 sorties were flown over Hamburg, during which 86 aircraft were lost and 174 damaged.[8]

The Hamburg raid was the first in the Second World War to firebomb a German city, and was followed later by similar raids on cities such as Dresden and Berlin. Hamburg was the first to be bombed as it was in reach of Allied bombers and also the second biggest manufacturing centre in Germany after Berlin, and the third largest port in the world after London' and New York. Five hundred thousand civilians are estimated to have been killed in these raids on German cities led by Air Chief Marshal Sir Arthur Harris of the RAF. The Hamburg raid probably killed members of the Godeffroy family. We learned that some elderly Godeffroys were still living in Hamburg at the time of our visit, but we decided not to intrude on them before we continued our journey to Poland, to visit Krakow and Auschwitz.

Margaret had always been keen to visit Auschwitz, the most notorious of the Holocaust death camps, where over one million, mostly Jewish, people died at the hands

---

8 'The Utility of Force' by General Sir Rupert Smith, Penguin – Allen Lane p 146 and 'The Berlin Diaries of Marie Vassiltchikov' Folio Society 1991

of the Nazis. This horror is depicted in the Academy Award winning movie "Schindler's List". We learned that there were actually two adjoining camps, Auschwitz and Birkenau. The former still exists consisting of brick two-story buildings that previously had been military barracks before becoming a prison. Auschwitz, and forty-five nearby sub-camps, housed workers for a range of local industries including the synthetic rubber works of I.G.Farben (split after the war into three chemical companies Bayer, Badische and Hoechst.) Birkenau, now demolished except for the notorious gate and entrance building, was the site of the early medical experiments and the death camp with its purpose-built gas chambers and crematoria. Prisoners would arrive by train from all over Europe, to be segregated on arrival and become either slave workers or dispatched immediately to their death. Our visit was silent and solemn as we were reminded that as we walked around the ground still contained human ash from the wartime crematoria!

Our stay in Cracow with its attractive central square softened our grim Polish visit, and churches packed with the faithful. Pope John the 23rd was born in a village near the city. My explorations and walks were limited because of arthritis but we had a wonderful driver to take us to nearby sights. He also showed us the apartment of Margaret's much-admired poet Wislawa Szymborska (who received the Nobel Prize for Literature in 1996). Margaret has since regretted that she did not knock on the door of the poet's apartment.

3

My Early childhood in Singapore

Reverting to my childhood, I have fond memories of the Heytman home in Singapore, at 92 Meyer Road. A large rambling and elevated house with lots of open living space, which included some rooms and a breezeway at ground level, rather like the raised houses one sees in Queensland.

The home was set well back from the road on a deep block of land, with the front of the house facing the sea and a grass lawn and some coconut palm trees ending in a stone sea wall some 5 to 6 feet high.

The sea view included islands on the horizon, some of which had villages as there were lights on these islands at night-time. As a child, I would look at those faraway lights and wonder who could be living there and what they might be doing. To one side of the large garden, on the roadside of the house, was a covered walkway leading to outbuildings that included the kitchen, storerooms, servants' quarters and a garage. I remember the house well, as from the time of my birth in March 1931, my mother and I would spend a month there each year with my grandmother on visits from Java.

Today the foreshore in front of the house has been reclaimed for the motorway from the city to Changi Airport (site of the prison used by the Japanese for prisoners of war in 1942-1945). Where once I would stand on the garden sea-wall, there is now a hedge screening the house from motorway traffic.

My childhood memories are of a constantly busy house with frequent comings and goings of visitors, and occasional visits with my mother, or grandmother, to the city centre or to the private Singapore Swimming Club. The latter was located on the coast near the then small airport midway between the house and the city. Apart from drinks enjoyed by the family at sunset on most days, a favourite evening pastime was Mah-jong, a Chinese game played with 144 small rectangular tiles which had intrigued me.

The repetitive clicks of the tiles as they were played, added to the game's intensity. Each player was dealt a number of tiles decorated with bamboos, circles or Chinese characters, and players kept the tiles hidden from opponents on a wooden stand. I very much regret that my mother sold the set made of ivory and kept in a leather case.

Living in Java, and Singapore, in those early colonial times was completely different to today. Not only were European colonials looked after by numerous servants who became part of the household, but one also became aware of the mysticism and religious beliefs of the Malay natives. I was told stories by the family of strange and unexplained happenings in my early childhood, including one occasion in my grandmother's house in Katong, when stones began falling from the ceiling.

The stones were sufficiently numerous to fill a wheelbarrow. A servant was sent to search the roof space above the ceiling and carried a gun, to investigate whether some inexplicable trick was being perpetrated. The servant stumbled on the rafters and shot himself in the leg accidentally, at which point the falling stones ceased. The servants explained that this happened because the appearance of blood had appeased the local spirit!

My family blamed the phenomenon on "poltergeists", those spirits believed by the Church at that time to be children who died unbaptised and went to limbo, caught between heaven and hell!

In Louis Couperus' book "The Hidden Force", there is reference to "a rain of stones that fell inside a house for sixteen days" in Sumedang Java, witnessed by a General of the Colonial Army A. V. Michiels. Such falling stones are also described in a book published in Java in 1926, which describes a number of similar occurrences.[9]

Another family story of such mysticism occurred when as a baby at my grandmother's Singapore house, my dummies kept disappearing. These reappeared after several days when my mother came to check on me in the nursery.

The missing dummies had fallen in a circle around my cot, and although the cot was covered with a mosquito net tucked under the mattress, my mouth and body were covered with soft white fluff. This incredible tale was repeated to me by my mother and also my aunts.

Anna Rosa in addition to running the homestead at

9 Falling Stones Excerpt from p 22. See Introduction Notes 49 and 50 in Couperus' book for further references to Javanese mysticism and religion.

92 Meyer Road also owned a business named Harmer & Company which operated a reservoir and water supply business to service and supply ships in Singapore's harbour.

The von Hartwig ship chandler company had bought this business in 1880, and being a monopoly, it was very profitable. The family sold their shares in Harmer & Company after the Second World War, in the late 1940s or early 1950s. This decision by Anna Rosa influenced by her three sons, was against the wishes of her daughters including my mother. As a child, I was never told of this transaction and have since reflected what would have eventuated if the family had retained the Company!

The Meyer Road residence was not the first home of Anna Rosa, having lived previously in Atjeh House, Orchard Road, Katong near the Sea View Hotel. In this earlier house she took in one or more boarders. This predated later more affluent days after her Godeffroy inheritance, when she moved to the Meyer Road house on the coast.

My grandfather, Hendrik Heytman, would have enjoyed his wife Anna Rosa's new wealth and became known in the Colony as a big game hunter. This took up an increasing amount of his time, probably leading to his retirement.

I remember as a young child during visits to Singapore, being asked to walk up and down, balancing on his legs, while he lay on a day sofa in the downstairs breezeway. This was to help alleviate pain in his legs following one of his hunting trips. I disliked this task finding it difficult to keep my balance. Although he was very appreciative of my efforts, he remained a distant figure, particularly as he was often away. My grandmother Anna Rosa whom I called "Gran", was however, always a loving presence and would spoil me endlessly. Could my grandfather's leg pains have been arthritis, which I have inherited? His reputation as a hunter of wild boar and tiger in Malaysia, was widely known in the Colony, and I was told that he joined Malaysian Sultans on their hunting trips.

My mother also claimed that Grandad had accompanied the Prince of Wales on a hunting trip when he visited Singapore in 1929, and also that she herself had danced with the Prince at a Gala Ball during his visit. Such stories were once again embellished by Mum and her family, as I was to discover repeatedly in later years.

In fact, I am mortified that grandfather Hendrik hunted and killed tigers, as they have become an endangered species and no longer exist in Malaysia.

Hendrik's carefree life of hunting would have become possible as a result of his wife's wealth. This may have preyed on him, as in 1934 at the age of 66 he committed suicide by shooting himself with his hunting rifle. My Mother told me that he suffered from depression and that he took his life following the death of his best friend. His suicide was an embarrassing family secret, and was never to be discussed and I became aware of his suicide only many years later.

My organised and capable grandmother soldiered on following Hendrik's death, overseeing the Harmer business as well as managing her large family.

Although having ample means she never sent her children to Europe for their education. She had received very limited education but more importantly, she had innate wisdom after a lifetime of overcoming difficulties.

I have speculated that she was frugal and financially cautious, having a husband who didn't work and who was, in fact, a drain on family resources. But what seems more likely, now that I reflect on the Heytman/Hagedorn history, is that the family was long established in Singapore and that my grandmother did not see herself as one of the colonial expatriates but as a local, born in Singapore, as was her mother. I followed the family tradition of being born on the island, as had my mother and her siblings. In contrast, my father with European roots, felt strongly about education, not having had this advantage himself. He insisted, therefore, that I be sent from Batavia to boarding school in Holland, when I turned 7 in 1938.

Sending children to European schools was the long established custom for expatriate colonials. My mother, and her brothers and sisters, were very sensitive and conscious that they had never completed their schooling in Europe, let alone attend a university. One can therefore sympathise with my mother's brothers, Willy and Bertie, who had married local Eurasians. I remember both of them complaining that their local education, and birth, had impeded their prospects in the Socony Standard Oil Company (now Exxon) for whom both worked in Singapore as accountants.

My mother Anna (known as "Jigs") was the third of the nine surviving children of Anna Rosa Heytman, two others Elsie and Erick not having survived childhood. My mother, Anna, was born 10th August 1903, in Atjeh House in Orchard Road Singapore, and died in Melbourne in 1987.

Her eldest brother was Willem Hendrik (1897 – 1967) known as "Willy", a gentle and kind man who loved our children, bringing them sweets when he would visit us in Hawthorn. Willy, who had retired to Melbourne before the war, was childless. He had a great interest in geraniums, becoming President of the Society. He would often bring us his latest blooms and varieties. Second in the family was Kathleen or "Kitty" (1898 – 1980) who married an Irish man Frank Atkins, neither of whom I ever met as they had moved to Cape Town, South Africa, before the war. Fourth was Harold (1904 – 1988) a powerful, tall man, who survived the notorious Burmese railway as a Japanese POW, and retired later to Sydney.

Next was Gertrude Alma (1906 – 2000) known as "Nan", married to an Englishman, Bernard Murcott, who had been the electrical engineer at Singapore's power station and who survived the war as a POW in Changi. The Murcotts retired to Perth after 1945 and their only child, Yvonne, married Paul Pell, a cousin of Cardinal Pell. Nan was my favourite and much loved aunt who supported me in Perth during my mother's illness. Sixth was Alice Louisa or "Poo" (1908 – 1980), the family beauty, married to Bevis La Cloche, living in Jersey, Channel Islands. Both had been POWs in Changi and Bevis ended the war as a slave labourer in Japan, having been shipped there from Singapore. Mum's youngest brother "Bertie" (1911 – 1998) escaped to Sydney before the fall of Singapore, and I visited him in 1949 after finishing school before starting university. Eighth was Eileen (1915 – 1987), a sweet generous woman and fantastic cook, particularly of curries. Her family lived modestly in a war time "Nissen Hut" in the hills east of Perth, looking after my grandmother, Anna Rosa.

Eileen was saintly and was burdened with her scoundrel Australian husband, Henry Drennan, who had worked on a tin dredge in Malaysia. He escaped before Singapore's fall in 1942 by seizing a boat intended for fleeing women and children, and worked later in Perth. The youngest of Mum's sisters was Dorothy Sylvia (1921 – 1992) who, after the war, married a Swiss engineer, Erwin Meyer, from St Gallen. They lived in Caracas Venezuela where he owned a concrete factory, and was the Swiss consul. They remained in Caracas after his retirement until they died, not wishing to leave their daughter Sylvia who was in prison on drug charges. Their other child Ricky was also imprisoned for drugs for several years before returning to Switzerland.

I very much regret that I did not take the opportunity to visit Dot and Irwin in Caracas during my ICI visits to South America in the late 1980's. They had been good to us during our early days in Oxford, and visited us later in England when we lived in St Albans.

4

My Father

My father had a very different background to my mother, having been born in Holland:

"Fortune had set it apart from other states and nations in Europe. It had become a world empire in two generations. As a formidable maritime economic power, it stretched across the globe from van Diemen's Land to … the archipelago group of islands north of Russia. But the Dutch were claustrophobic circumnavigators. All that power and wealth was, in the end, sucked into the cramped space between the Scheldt and the Ems Rivers: a swarming beehive of fewer than two million people."[10]

The Dutch had a long history of early voyages and exploration in the Far East and Pacific. Their first entry to the area was with the "Druyfken", or little pigeon, which sailed through Torres Strait and landed on the East coast of the Gulf of Carpentaria in 1595. There were many subsequent Dutch voyages, particularly when the spice

---

10 'The Embarrassment of Riches – an Interpretation of Dutch Culture in the Golden Age' by Simon Schama, Harper Collins 1991

trade was developed in the Mollucca islands. This trade based on pepper, cloves, mace, cinnamon and nutmeg the most desired and expensive, was highly profitable. Some early voyages ended as shipwrecks on the West Australian coast, the most famous and notorious being that of the "Batavia".[11]

The wrecks occurred because ships followed Easterly trade winds to Australia after rounding South Africa's cape.

Batavia was established as the regional headquarters of the Dutch East Indies Company in March 1619 by Jan Pieterszoon Coen on the site of a small Dutch fort and the Javanese port Jacatra (now Jakarta).

The Dutch choice of this name was derived from the Germanic tribe 'Batavi', who were first encountered by the Romans. The tribe inhabited a muddy fertile peninsula between the Rhine and Waal rivers, some miles south of what is now the city of Utrecht. The Batavi put up a heroic resistance against Julius Caesar and his legions, under general Claudius Civilis.

The Dutch were to take a step of major commercial importance when they created a business model which was to become the foundation of modern capitalism. In 1602 they established a chartered company, the Vereenigde Oost-Indische Compagnie (The Dutch East Indies Company) known as VOC. This was given a monopoly in all trading matters with quasi-sovereign rights to build forts, maintain armed forces and set up administrative systems of government.

It was the first company to issue stock to shareholders, and arguably the world's first megacorporation.

---

11 'The First and Last Voyage of the Batavia', Philippe Gosard. 1993

It paid an annual dividend of 18% for almost 200 years!

Following the 1782 Treaty of Paris which ended the European war, the Dutch trading monopoly in the Far East was broken and their share of the spice trade dwindled. Despite new plantation crops of coffee, tea and quinine, the VOC finally became bankrupt and its commission expired in 1799 when the Dutch Government took over the VOC's territories as colonial possessions.

When Napoleon annexed the Netherlands in 1810, the Dutch supremacy throughout the Far East was destroyed, and Sir Stamford Raffles then occupied and administered Java for ten years. At the end of the Napoleonic wars, the British returned Java to the Dutch, and in exchange obtained Malacca in Malaysia in 1824. The Dutch were finally compelled to leave Batavia in 1949 when the city reverted to the Javanese name of the 17th century fishing village which adjoined the earlier Dutch fort called Jayakarta, the name meaning "victorious and prosperous". The name has been modernised by Indonesia today to 'Jakarta'.

The former Dutch East Indies, now Indonesia since 1949, comprises a "necklace of more than thirteen thousand dazzling tropical islands lying across and south of the Equator, north of Australia." The islands stretch a distance equivalent to that from Broome in Western Australia to Christchurch in New Zealand.

"Indonesia is the fourth most populous nation on earth after China, India and the United States. It is the largest Islamic nation in the world with a population of two hundred and twenty million embracing some three hundred ethnic groups and two hundred and fifty distinct languages. Java is Indonesia's most densely populated island."[12]

And what is the Dutch residue of 350 years of colonial rule? As noted by Cees Nooteboom:

"It is almost as if all we left behind in our former colonies is a scattering of gravestones and churches. Our language has dissipated, evaporated, blown away from the Indonesian archipelago. Was it all too far from home?" [13]

In contrast to the Spanish and Portuguese language and literature in South America, which gave the old languages in Europe a "Breath of Fresh Air".[14]

The Dutch government organisation administering Java in the 1920s and 1930s was the one under which my father, and his elder brother Joop both worked. At the end of the war in 1945 the Dutch attempted to restore their colonial rule in a war that involved Dutch troops fighting Indonesian nationalists. This was a doomed, fruitless and ill-conceived exercise, and the Dutch were forced to withdraw following economic pressure from the United States. The latter were opposed to colonialism fearing that the Indonesian revolution might lurch towards communism.[15]

Dad, named Joannes Marie, and known as Jan, was born in Amsterdam during the final years of the Dutch empire,

12 'Krakatoa' by Simon Winchester, 2003, p 29 & 141

13 'Roads to Santiago' by Cees Nooteboom, p 245

14 'Dutch Culture Overseas – Colonial Practice in the Netherlands Indies 1900-1942' Francis Gouda, Amsterdam 1992, p 237

15 'The Indonesian National Revolution 1945 -1950', A.J.S.Reid. Sydney 1974

on 25th November 1902. He grew up as fourth child in a large, typically disciplined Dutch family of thirteen children, nine of which were boys and four girls. Dad's early childhood during the First World War would have been difficult. The war started in August 1914, when he was not yet 12, and ended in November 1918, when he was a 16 year old teenager.

Joannes Marie (Jan) at age 16.

Although Holland remained neutral throughout the war, the population suffered hardship as a result of the naval blockade by the English who were suspicious of the Dutch, believing they may have been supporting the Germans. The blockade resulted in major shortages of food and coal in Holland, so that Dad and his family would have been cold and hungry throughout the war.

The only record I have of these years was an injury Dad suffered as a teenager, a result of a train accident near

Weesp on the 13 September 1918. I do not know why he made this journey, but after the train wreck he walked along the railway track to his home in Amsterdam, a distance of over 80 miles. This was quite a feat for an injured teenager, showing great determination and fortitude. The early picture of Dad is of a hardened tough young man, experienced in deprivation and equipped to meet the future challenges he would face when he left his home in Holland for the Far East. It took courage to set off alone on a long sea voyage to distant Java, although the island was well known being part of the Spice Islands which had made Holland rich.

The Dutch economy and access to their colonies in the Far East were seriously affected by the 1914 - 1918 war, leading to widespread unemployment, and this probably influenced Dad to seek opportunities in the Dutch East Indies as he left home as a teenager without completing secondary schooling and minimal savings, and it is possible that he would have worked his passage to Java. Did he leave Amsterdam on his own or with a friend? Either way, it would have been challenging parting from his family to board a ship in Amsterdam and set sail for the Orient.

After arriving in Java he obtained employment on a quinine plantation in Bandung, located in the volcanic mountains south of Batavia. Java had become the quinine capital of the world and jobs were available in this growth industry with quinine as the only known remedy for malaria at the time.

Quinine was the first effective treatment for malaria in the 17th century. It had long been used by the Quechua

Indians of Peru, derived from the ground bark of cinchona trees. Its first use in Europe was to treat malaria in Rome in 1631, as malaria was endemic there because of the swamps and marshes surrounding the city, and the Jesuit Salumbrino had observed its use in Lima. It was known initially as Jesuit's bark. To maintain their monopoly on the bark from cinchona saplings, Peru began outlawing its export. The Dutch government persisted in smuggling the seeds, and by the 1930s Dutch plantations in Java were producing 22 million pounds of bark, or 97% of the world's quinine production. Quinine played a significant role in the colonization of Africa and was regarded as the prime reason Africa ceased to be known as "the white man's grave".

Dad's work on the plantation in Java would have been extremely arduous and challenging in the sweltering and humid conditions. Production of quinine from tree bark involved a number of stages. It was essential to first build earth terraces on the steep mountain slopes in order to minimise erosion and avoid collection of stagnant water. Shaded nursery seed beds were then built for the young seedlings which were watered with a mist spray to avoid fungus diseases.

After two years the seedlings were transferred and planted in friable soil of the terraced plantation. After a further four to five years the plantation would be thinned out, and a final harvest of the bark yielding quinine occurs some fifteen to eighteen years after the initial planting.

The harvested trees are cut up into short logs before the bark is stripped. Following initial drying in the sun, any residual water in the bark is driven off in drying ovens and finally then broken into small chips for shipment.

The whole process from initial planting is repeated every year to maintain continuous production of quinine from the plantation.

Dad probably worked in several of these production stages. He would have become familiar with the Javanese language and have adjusted to exotic spicy food with few, if any, amenities.

It would have been a complete change from his life in Holland. Instead of the well-ordered and clean family home in Amsterdam, he now lived in a primitive "atap" or palm tree leaf hut, with nearby jungle infested with leeches, poisonous snakes, chattering monkeys, tropical birds and the ever present ant and scorpion insects. The dark nights with the pungent smell of decaying vegetation, buzzing mosquitos and strange sounds from the jungle would have been a challenging backdrop for the young Dutchman.

The quinine property where Dad worked was run by a Dutchman named Kees Heytman, whose brother named Hendrik lived in Singapore.

Unbeknown to Dad, the latter was to become his future father-in-law. The brothers relationship led to Dad meeting the Heytman family and my mother when he moved later from Java to Singapore.Following his initial employment on the quinine estate at Pangli Pogali near Bandung, Dad worked briefly in Batavia for Coats Paton, a textile trading company. This involved much easier office and sales work in a bustling colonial city with many amenities and distractions.

In 1927 once again seeking new opportunities at the age of 25 and after working eight years in Java, Dad sailed to Singapore on a Dutch KPM steamer ("Koninklijke Paketvaart Maatschappij" or "Royal Shipping Company"), and found employment as a Singer Sewing Machine salesman.

It is likely that the cotton textile firm in Batavia would have provided Dad a reference and contact for the Singapore Company.

At that time Mum was working as a secretary at the Singer Company in the Chartered Bank of India building in Singapore, and Dad is likely to have met her there when he joined the company. There was also the very direct relationship of the brothers Kees and Hendrik Heytman, the former being Dad's earlier employer in Java. It is therefore not surprising and perhaps inevitable that Dad became a boarder in my grandmother's home in Atjeh House. This was yet another major change for Dad who now found himself in a household of nine children, including six daughters, then aged 29 to 6. It was not long before a relationship developed between Dad and the second oldest daughter, my mother Anna.

According to Mum's sister Nan, this good-looking tall Dutchman with a broad smile and blue eyes was popular with the Heytman girls. In less than two years after his arrival in Singapore, Mum and Dad, aged 25 and 26, were married by Father Ruadel at the Cathedral of the Good Shepherd on the 25th January 1929. They left the following day for Kuala Lumpur where they lived for one year, returning to Singapore where I was born on 10th March 1931. Dad unfortunately lost his job with the Singer Company six weeks after my birth because of the Depression, and this would have devastated the young couple.

After several months of unemployment, the small Lochtenberg family left Singapore on the "Christian Huygens" steamship for Holland in September 1931.

It would have been difficult and uncomfortable for Dad, newly married and with a baby, to be jobless and living in Singapore with his mother-in-law, my grandmother Anna Rosa. He would not have enjoyed imposing on her, and would have hoped that the chances of employment in Holland might be better.

However he was to be disappointed, as he continued to remain jobless for the next two years with the family of three living with Dad's parents in Amsterdam at Nassau Kade 173. It was an exceptionally strained time for my parents, not only for Dad but also for my mother who has told me she was very unhappy living in the home of her Dutch in-laws, with a new baby and an out of work husband.

And Dad would have been miserable, burdening his parents during the Depression and returning each day without a job. Meanwhile as a baby, I was blissfully unaware of my parents' problems.

In 1933, Dad's elder brother Joop, who was then working in Java for the Dutch East Indies Tin Commission wrote to Dad telling him there were jobs available in Batavia. So once again Dad set out seeking employment in the Far East.

We left Holland on the "SS Johann van Olden Barneveldt". The family travelled "steerage", which is 3rd class and takes its name from cabins being below waterline near the rudder and noisy propellers.

Our fares for this return voyage to Singapore were paid by my grandmother Anna Rosa.

Back in Singapore my mother and I lived with my grandmother Anna Rosa, and Mum was able to get a secretarial job with SMN (Nederlandse Stoomvaart Maatschapij), a Dutch shipping company. Dad went on alone to Java and lived with Joop, his older brother in Batavia while he tried to re-establish himself.

In time he managed to get a job "at the bottom of the ladder at a very low salary" according to Mum. A year later in 1934 after this enforced family separation Mum and I joined Dad in Batavia. Dad's new job was with "Carl Schlieper", a German trading company which imported steel products to Java and the Dutch East Indies.

Dad made good progress in the firm, no doubt driven by hard work and his determination to succeed after a long period of unemployment. He was made a Director of the company in 1935, and a picture in April 1937 shows Dad standing, making a speech at a Company dinner in Batavia attended by a member of the Schlieper family who were the private owners of the Company.

Interestingly, the photo shows a picture of Adolf Hitler, then Chancellor of Germany, on the dining room wall. The photo also shows an ashtray and cigarette at the seat of every person attending the dinner, as smoking was very fashionable and widespread at that time.

Jan Lochtenberg making a speech
at a company dinner, 1937.

Mum and Dad each smoked a "Capstan" tin of 50 cigarettes every day! My "secondary smoking" daily of 100 cigarettes, perhaps explains why I was never attracted to smoking when I grew up. I remember the round Capstan tins with their sealed tops of aluminium foil, which my parents allowed me to open by rotating the lid,which cuts the foil seal. Every tin included a picture card of the English Royal family and the coronation of George VI. I collected these cards and pasted them in a book supplied by Capstan, now long lost!

Although having never completed his schooling, Dad was energetic and clearly intelligent, as demonstrated by his rapid advance in the "Schlieper" Company prior to the war. Dad spoke fluent English and was also proficient in German, French and Chinese, and of course Malay. His lack of formal education no doubt made him appreciate its importance, and his later insistence that I be educated by the Jesuits.

I remember Dad being a very proud Dutchman who was resolute and determined. Being the third son in a large family he developed relationships easily and had a good sense of humour. I remember him often making others laugh, with a sharp or interesting comment. He was a devout Catholic with strong beliefs and values. He never worked with his hands after the early quinine plantation, and was comfortable in an office setting. His main interests were books, politics and opera.

Dad was tall (190cms), wore size 12 shoes and was well built but somewhat overweight. He was demanding and short tempered if things were not done the way he expected. It is perhaps not surprising that this interesting and restless man was to marry a "foreigner" in a strange Far Eastern land far away from his European roots and family.

5

Childhood in Java & New York

From the age of 2 to 7, I lived with my parents in Batavia at 21 Villalaan (now Jalan Cendana in Jakarta), in the same street and a few doors from Dad's brother Joop, who was working in the Tin Commission for the Government.

Joop and his wife Corrie (formerly Offerman) had three boys Ben ("Big Ben" or "Groote Ben"), Jan and Hans. Ben was two years older than me, Jan being six months older, and Hans two years younger.

Left to Right: Jan, Ben (author), Big Ben (back) and Hans.

The four of us were inseparable, going to the same school and playing but inevitably also fighting together. Our favourite indoor game was 'Monopoly' but this often ended with accusations of cheating. Living my early childhood years near three cousins meant I did not suffer the full effect of being an only child.

One of my sharpest memories of our home in Villalaan is of the gravel drive adjoining the house. Being gravel meant I would hear Dad's car when he arrived home after work, especially on those days when I had been naughty. Mum would say,

"Wait till your father comes home" and would make me wait for his arrival in a small pantry room near the kitchen. Finally after hearing the crunch of Dad's car on the gravel I would hear Dad and Mum's distant voices, and finally Dad's appearance often followed by a spanking. Despite these punishments, I adored my father who for me walked ten feet tall, and I always knew he loved me dearly.

The garden of our home was full of birds and the fragrant smells of tropical plants and flowers, and in the evening the roar of cicadas. There were also frogs, bats and lizards.

Inside the house one would sometimes disturb small lizards high up on the walls called "tjetjaks", who were harmless and ate insects. During the day one would also hear the sound of street vendors and their carts calling out their sale of food or fruit, and services such as sharpening of knives and scissors.

On weekdays I was not allowed to leave the table until I had finished my meal. As I hated some meals I would empty my plate through a nearby window until caught one day which resulted in a spanking.

But I loved my favourite desert called "floating islands", of whipped egg-white floating on a lake of custard. On weekends the family dinners were usually "Rijstafel" or fried rice "Nasi Goring", the former being a range of curries and "sambals" made of chilies and spice dishes. On Saturday nights our nearby Lochtenberg relatives would often visit us. Dad and his brother Joop would end the evening on the verandah, drinking Bols Gin from a brown stone bottle, discussing family events and world affairs.

Dad was an avid reader with wide interests, and had many books lining a wall of his study which were his special joy. On the wall above his desk was a large map of China, on which he would mark the advance of the Japanese army in their 1930s war with China. He would go to his study every night and follow the progress of the war, which concerned him greatly, on the radio.

The Imperial Japanese Army had been fighting the Chinese on the mainland since 1931, having initially occupied and later annexed Manchuria. In 1937 they invaded and conquered Beijing and incendiary bombed Shanghai. They massacred 250,000 Chinese in Nanking alone. In the eight years from 1937 to 1945 the Chinese lost 14 million whereas the United States and the British Empire each lost 400,000 during the Second World War. Little did my father realise then that the Japanese he was so concerned about would one day claim his own life as a prisoner of war in 1945.

In 2008, Margaret and I visited Nanjing and were moved and overcome by the city's memorial museum recording the Japanese war crimes.

At the museum entrance is a dramatic twenty metres tall statue of a woman crying out and clutching her dead child.

Dad's library contained many reference books including what I called the "Gundru" books with pictures of dinosaurs. Sometimes as a treat he would allow me to look at these as well as other books. I loved entering his study, but was not allowed to do so unless he was present. Dad sparked my interest in stars and our galaxy The Milky Way and he would sometimes take me into the garden at night and point out constellations such as Orion's belt, and how planets were brighter and did not flicker like the stars. He would test me to see if I could locate "Pisces" the fish, "Cancer" the crab, or "Sagitarius" the archer.

To this day I have had an interest and fascination with astronomy and astrophysics·

I had my own playroom along the back corridor, where I had a large collection of lead soldiers, guns and carriages, as well as a German Marklin train set out on the floor. The train on its tracks would occupy me for hours, and these happy memories led me recently to buy a Marklin railway engine at a Melbourne auction. As a result of these toy interests, my birthday and Christmas presents were often another regiment of soldiers or a new railway signal or carriage.

Our servants included a cook or "kokkie", a maid or "babu", a head steward called "Tuan", a gardener, and later when Dad became a company Director, a driver for our first car, a Vauxhall, and most importantly for my early childhood a nursemaid or "Amah". Some of the servants would return at night to their homes in the "Kampongs" or nearby villages, but a few lived with their families at the rear of our house. As a child I was close to and knew the servants extremely well and spoke fluent Indonesian to them. I spoke English to my mother, but when my father arrived home the family would usually speak Dutch. It is of course relatively easy to pick up a language when you are a child!

School was close to our home and was run by Jesuits and again called St Louis. I remember my First Communion as I was chosen to speak on behalf of the class. Instead of the occasion being very special, it was a disaster as I had drunk some water before Mass and was not allowed to make my first Communion that day, having unwittingly broken my fast then a strict Catholic rule! The church, St Theresa in Theresakerk Weg, was walking distance from our home.

An early memory of my Java childhood was on a public holiday, which included an evening fireworks celebration with family and friends. I let off a rocket that made straight for Dad, burning a hole in the seat of his trousers. Happily he didn't suffer serious injury, but I do remember his burned trousers and reaction!

My early childhood in Java included trips each year with my mother to the Heytman home in Singapore to visit my grandmother Anna Rosa.

During one such visit I celebrated my 7th birthday on the Meyer Road front lawn facing the sea. I recall visiting Uncle Willy's Singapore home, and being fascinated with his fully equipped home workshop full of machinery and tools. Was this an early hint of my later interest in engineering?

In March 1939 Dad went on long-service leave with Mum to Europe and also to take me to boarding school in Holland. We sailed on the Nord Deutscher Lloyd Bremen German ship S.S. "Scharnhorst" for Europe. The ship was named after the brilliant anti-Bonapartist Prussian general Gerhard von Scharnhorst who was killed in 1813 at Lutzen fighting Napoleon's Grand Armee.[16] Scharnhorst initiated a reform of the Prussian army having studied the military changes made by Napoleon, who had achieved remarkable and continuous successes against European armies until the battle of Waterloo in 1815. The name was also given to a famous German battleship sunk in Wold War 2.

It is interesting that Dad booked passage on a German and not Dutch ship, but perhaps not surprising as his Company was German owned. Shipboard life lasted several weeks and included fancy dress parties, "horse races" (where passengers competed by reeling in wooden horses mounted on wheels), deck sports such as throwing coits or shuffleboard. I was also "baptised" by Neptune and his helpers in the ship's swimming pool when we crossed the equator. I remember being scared having to stand before Neptune and then being dunked by his assistants in the pool. During the voyage I also visited the bridge and the cavernous engine room with its large and noisy machinery. The trip was a huge adventure for me and I have since continued a life-long interest in ships and books about travel.

I started boarding school at St Louis in Amersfoort with my three Lochtenberg cousins from Batavia.

16 'Napoleon' Paul Johnson 2002, p 146

We disembarked from the "Scharnhorst" in Rotterdam, and took a train to Amsterdam where a large group of the Lochtenberg family were at the station to greet us.

It was clearly a very special family occasion to welcome back my father from the Far East colonies. He must have been proud returning with a job and family, and his body language reveals this in the many photographs taken that day at the station.

The Lochtenberg Family reunited
(Jan Lochtenberg 3rd from the left)

We stayed with Dad's elder sister Lijda (his favourite sibling), her husband Han and their children.

Han was a very strict Dutch father, and at dinner during our stay when we children made too much noise he would bellow,

"Allemaal naar de wasskamer!" ("Everyone to the laundry!") while slamming his clenched fist on the table. His children and I would quietly troop out to the laundry, where we remained until called back.

My grandparents Bernardus Johannes Marie (born 15th March 1872) and Maria Dorothea Lochtenberg (nee Ruhe born 7th April 1875) hosted a celebratory lunch soon after our arrival, at their home at Schepenlaan 5, Amsterdam.

Their home was very "Dutch" being spotlessly clean and tidy with everything in its place, and with holy pictures on walls in every room. Even to my young eyes it was clear that Oma Maria Dorothea was the stronger of my two grandparents and that she ruled the family. Grandfather Bernardus Lochtenberg's working career had been with a company which provided insurance cover for all Catholic churches and properties in Holland. I suspect that by the time of our visit in 1939 he may have been retired. Uncle Joop, Corrie and their 3 boys, also arrived at that time from Java, and all Dad's brothers and sisters were at the lunch – a very special gathering of the Lochtenberg family.

The memories I have of my short stay as a boarder at St Louis Jesuit School in Amersfoort in the spring and early summer of 1939 were very happy ones. I remember weekends spent building sand castles and digging tunnels in a large nearby sand pit play area with my classmates, and searching for blueberries in the nearby woods on Sundays.

Mum and Dad took long service leave to visit France and Germany as well as relations in Holland. Photographs show them clearly enjoying their time in Paris, and there is a picture of Dad in a light-hearted mood photographed with Mum sitting in an airplane. They later went to Dad's German steel suppliers in the Ruhr and the head office of his Company "Carl Schlieper".

It was during these business visits in Germany that Dad would have been warned about taking his son out of Holland.

German factories had by then been converted to produce war equipment such as tanks instead of tractors. In the previous year of 1938, Austria had been re-united with Gemany in the "Anschluse", and Nazis openly attacked Jewish businesses in the 'Kristalnacht Pogrom'.

These events must have worried Dad having entered his son in boarding school and this prompted him to leave Holland with his family when Germany invaded Poland. Dad by then had a history of travelling across the world, and did not delay in collecting me from school and driving through the night to Rotterdam port.

Although Mum and I then escaped the war by sailing to Singapore, Dad travelled separately across the Atlantic to New York to open a "Schlieper" buying operation. He was thereby able to source US steel products instead of from Germany for shipment to his Company in Java. This New York sourcing initiative must have been discussed by Dad with the "Schlieper Company" and family owners during his visit to Germany.

Despite warnings Dad received in Germany of the forthcoming war, surprisingly they did not intrude in the summer of 1939 on the family holiday in Jersey at the end of my school term. Dad hired a car and with Mum and me drove through Belgium to France. My only memory of any signs of the impending war, was the tension and delay we experienced in crossing border check-points between Holland, Belgium and France.

The trip included a visit to the island monastery of Mont St Michel, and then via Amiens to St Malo to catch a ferry to Jersey. There we visited Bevis La Cloche and his wife, Mum's sister Alice known as "Poo".

In Jersey we also met up with my grandmother Anna Rosa, and Mum's sisters Dorothy and Nan, who had come to Europe to share a family holiday. The photos of this Jersey visit do not include Nan's husband Bernard, as he had remained in Singapore.

I remember the Jersey holiday as idyllic with many beach picnics and my excitement at meeting Poo's son Hugh, who was older than me and was swim champion of Jersey. Aunt Nan's young daughter, Yvonne was also there. The get-together was literally the calm before the storm.

Unbeknown to me as an 8-year-old, Dad probably urged his mother-in-law and sisters-in-law of the need to leave Europe which would soon be engulfed in a war with Germany.

All the family members gathered in Jersey, including 'Poo' and Bevis, left Europe at the end of that summer for Singapore, where they were captured subsequently by the Japanese or able to escape to Australia.

Dad drove Mum and me to Rotterdam to embark on the "S.S.Dempo" which sailed for Cape Town. The ship travelled at maximum speed as there was widespread fear of German submarines. The family was very fortunate to escape from Holland which was to suffer greatly under German occupation. Even in 1945 in the very last year of the war, the Dutch experienced repeated heavy Allied bombing as well as starvation and ongoing persecution by German occupying forces.

The "Dempo" ended its voyage in Singapore where Mum and I joined Gran at Meyer Road and I had my 9th birthday.

We lived there for a year until we were able to leave to join my father in the United States. We sailed on the Dutch ship the "SS Klipfontein" from Singapore in August 1940 across the Pacific to Portland, Oregon. I would have attended a school during my year in Singapore, but I have virtually no recollection of this period, except that it was a very unsettled time with Dad on the other side of the world in New York, the continuing war in Europe, and Mum and I waiting anxiously for the day when the family could be reunited in New York.

After a surprising uneventful and pleasant voyage across the Pacific, Mum and I travelled from Portland across the United States on a train named the "Oregon Rosë".

The journey took several days with nights spent in "Pullman" beds made up by black stewards. Dad joined the train somewhere between Chicago and New York as he was very keen to see us after our long separation.

The next fifteen months in the United States were very happy ones, living in an apartment Dad rented on 72nd Street on the East Side, and New York became my playground. Rides on the subway were then a nickel (5 cents) as was a child's movie ticket at Loew's Theatre near our apartment building. The full movie programme usually started with someone playing an organ, followed by a "Movietone" newsreel mainly about the European war, a secondary film (perhaps starring Ronald Reagan, later to become President!), a cartoon and finally the feature film.

On weekends, I would sail my toy boat on a lake in

Central Park, and I remember the "L" elevated railway along 2nd or 3rd street. Dad would take me for walks also on the weekends in Central Park and sometimes as far as Harlem with its vibrant black community, which in those days was safe and a very interesting way to spend an afternoon.

However it would be many months after our arrival before I was allowed to leave our block and cross the street by myself! I developed a hobby building model planes from balsa kits, and model warships, which I painted grey. I also learned fretwork, cutting out designs from plywood, and amazingly today still have one of these small "oriental" pieces which I made in New York. I no doubt developed these hobbies as I had no siblings and had become separated from my three Dutch cousins whom I grew up with; any friends I made at school were scattered throughout New York City.

The school I attended was St Anne's Academy run by Marist Brothers, on 5th Avenue at 76th street. Hemmed in by city buildings, our only sportsground was on nearby Randall's Island where was held the school's annual Sports Day. The school has since been moved to Long Island.

I studied the piano although I would have much preferred the drums but Dad said this would be too noisy for our apartment.

My school results improved progressively as Dad and Mum gave me an incentive reward system. Achieving good behaviour and marks at school led to additional pocket money which I spent on comics such as Dick Tracey, Batman and Superman. Dick Tracey amazed me as he wore a wristwatch which he would speak to. A forerunner of today's mobile phone!

In the summer holidays of 1941, Mum and Dad sent me to a camp named St John's on Hunter Lake near Parksville in the Catskills Mountains north of New York. After living in the confines of Manhattan, I enjoyed the liberating and open-air experience of the camp. I think I was away about a month, living in one of several wooden bungalows, each housing eight boys and a senior councillor. The camp was directed by priests and run like an army establishment but it was great fun.

I learned to fire a 0.22 rifle, how to paddle a canoe on the camp lake, first aid and proficiency levels of swimming - which included recovering a large rock in 10 feet of water, as well as having to fight a boxing match. I failed as a boxer, as early in my fight I took a blow on the nose and had to retire bleeding. I also went horse riding and learned archery. At night after dinner we would sit in a circle around a large open fire toasting marshmallows, listening to stories read by one of the young men who were our camp councillors.

I have memories of my parents taking me to the 1940 "World of Tomorrow" World Fair built on a reclaimed rubbish dump near the newly opened "La Guardia" Airport, named after the then mayor of New York.

One vivid memory of the Fair was seeing Esther Williams dive from a high tower into an open-air pool. The chairman of the Fair's science advisory committee incredibly was Albert Einstein, who then aged 60 had lost his home, savings, nationality and was divorced from his wife!

My eyes opened wide when Dad took me to the "Barnum and Bailey" Circus at Madison Square Garden, to see a line of 50 elephants, each trunk holding the tail of the one in front, and also lion-tamers, trapeze artists, equestrian acts and clowns. The show opened an hour before the performance began, when we went to see the animals in their cages including lions and tigers. I enjoyed this treat very much and also some weekend visits to Westchester up the Hudson River. Dad had friends there called Law.

In winter I would toboggan down the Law's snow covered property called Briarcliff Manor. Dad had made friends with a number of well-to-do people through his business dealings. Some of these mistakenly believed we were wealthy, as Dad's business involved large purchases of steel products for shipment to the Dutch East Indies. (This was of course on behalf of the "Schlieper Company".)

At the start of the war the Company was appropriated by the Dutch East Indies Government, and renamed "Java Staal" ("Java Steel"). In New York Dad looked very much a successful businessman as shown in a winter picture of him standing on a high balcony of the Empire State Building.

He is looking at the camera with a confident calm gaze, dressed in a heavy overcoat and felt hat. He must have thought that he had finally achieved some success after his many early years of hardship and unemployment.

It was about this time that I became somewhat aware of some tension between Mum and Dad. I learned many years later from my Aunt Nan that Dad desperately wanted a second child but he learned that Mum had independently taken steps to avoid becoming pregnant again.

Dad while in New York became interested in American politics and a great admirer of Wendel Wilkie, the

Republican nominee for President in 1940. However Wilkie was well beaten by the third term Democrat incumbent President Franklin Roosevelt. It was a tense time with news of the war in Europe, which the United States had yet to join. My parents however enjoyed attending the opera and I recall their favourites being "La Traviata" and "Cavelliera Rusticana".

Dad also followed boxing, Joe Louis being an American idol having beaten the German champion Max Smelling for the world heavy weight title. Boxing then had not degenerated into pervasive corruption and "fragmented titles so that almost anyone wearing gloves was recognised as a champ by some body or other"[17]

In the autumn of 1941 on October 4th, Dad, Mum and I left New York for Batavia, Java. It was clearly meant to be an extended business trip with the family intending to return to New York, as our furniture and my toys were put into storage. Our trip to Java was quite an expedition. We first moved from our apartment to the Lexington Hotel in New York (which became derelict in the 1980s), while our furniture was packed for storage. We began our journey from La Guardia by United Airlines "Mainliner Flight 3", stopping in Chicago.

During this flight to the West Coast, our plane was forced down in Cheyenne where we had to stay the night to avoid a thunderstorm. Our DC 4 plane was not pressurised and therefore unable to fly above storms.

In San Francisco we stayed at the Clift Hotel (which in the 1990s has been updated to become a luxury boutique

17 Financial Times, 27-28 March 2010

hotel) and the next stage of our journey from San Francisco to Java was on the Dutch ship MV "Noordam".

On arrival in Batavia we rented a house in Tjandjoerweg and I remember purchases of some furniture by the family. I was allowed to bring a few of my toy soldiers from New York but little else. I was back once again in a Dutch school, joining my cousins Ben, Jan and Hans who had returned from Holland in September 1939. However the Japanese attack of Pearl Harbour on the 7th December 1941 ended the plans my parents had of returning to New York.

An hour and twenty minutes before the attack on Pearl Harbour, Japanese soldiers began wading ashore at Kota Bahru on the North East coast of Malaya. The Allies were not able to stem the Japanese advance down the Malay Peninsula towards Singapore.

"With an Arisaka rifle slung over his shoulders, a ration of fish and rice balls in his pack and rubber-soled boots on his feet, the Japanese infantryman pedalled furiously southward on his bicycle. Artillery and tanks followed along the paved roads, mending blown-up bridges. In front of them swept a human tide of Allied soldiers and civilians, all desperate to escape captivity and heading for Singapore."[18]

Malaya and Singapore defended by 130,000 British, Indian and Australian forces were captured in only ten weeks by 60,000 Japanese soldiers in February 1942 in a humiliating Allied disaster.

My grandmother Anna Rosa, having returned from her pre-war European holiday, lived in Singapore until January 1942.

---

18 'Kill the Tiger', Peter Thompson and Robert Macklin, Hodder 2002. p 42

The Japanese entered Kuala Lumpur on January 12th and Singapore surrendered on February 15th following heavy bombardment - which led to shortages of food and water.

Gran and my Aunt Dorothy were able to escape from Singapore and stay briefly with us in Batavia. I remember visits then by Dorothy's boyfriend Basil Gotto, a RAF pilot relocated from Singapore to Java, who joined us for several evening family meals. After a short and increasingly anxious stay, Gran and Dorothy left Batavia for Perth, Australia, where Mum and I later joined them.

Anna Rosa continued then living in Perth at her daughter Eileen's house in Parkerville until Eileen died in 1963.

When Gran and Dorothy joined us in Batavia, Japanese bombing air-raids had become a daily event. Alerted by sirens, we would go to our air-raid shelter, which was one of the storerooms at the rear of the house along the covered passage to the kitchen and servants' quarters.

Dad had the shelter made by having a wooden room built inside the brick walls, and the gap between the bricks and timber filled with sand. This shelter would not withstand a direct hit by a bomb but would protect us from shrapnel and bullets. The room was stocked with supplies, but we soon tired of sitting in the shelter as the Japanese bombers attacked distant targets, bypassing the suburbs where we lived.

I would watch the planes flying high in the sky like silver birds, and sometimes after a dogfight see a plane spiralling down trailing smoke. Not that there was any serious opposition to the Japanese planes.

Dad took me on one occasion to the central square, in Batavia called Koning's Plein (King's Square), which was surrounded by trees on four sides. Koningsplein (called 'Gambir' in Malay) was the largest and most fashionable square in colonial Batavia. It was a large grassed space about a kilometre square. Colonial society would gather there in the evenings, and in earlier days would parade around in their carriages. The official city residence of the Governor General (who usually lived in Buitenzorg, now called Bogor, in the mountains) was on Koningsplein as were government buildings, clubs, consulates, and a few large private residences.

Under the trees in Koningsplein square I now saw the bodies of "Hurricane" fighter planes, without their wings. Dad told me that the Allies had sent plane reinforcements to Java by ship, but incredibly sent the fuselages in one ship, and the wings in another. The second ship was sunk by the Japanese, so that the aircraft bodies lay useless and a constant reminder of the Allied blunder!

At about this time, Dad was enlisted as a private for military service, as any Dutchman below the age of 40 was conscripted into the Dutch East Indies Army, and Dad was 39 (Born 25th Nov. 1902). If Dad had left Java then he would have been court martialled.

Most of Mum's other family had lived in Singapore before the war. Her sisters Nan and Eileen escaped to Perth before the fall of Singapore. Eileen's Australian husband Henry, who had worked on a Malaysian tin mine, turned up unexpectedly in Perth in March 1942. Other family members caught by the Japanese in Singapore and interned in Changi Prison were Nan's husband, Bernard Murcott, who for the remainder of the war worked as an Electrical Engineer in Singapore's Power Station. Also in Changi was Mum's brother Harold, who was sent later to the infamous Burmese railway where all his teeth were knocked out by a Japanese camp guard for insubordination.

Harold's wife Elsie escaped from Singapore and settled in Sydney. Harold joined her there after the war and they lived there until their deaths. Mum's sister Alice (known as 'Poo') and husband Bevis La Cloche were interned in Singapore but Bevis ended the war working as a prisoner in a factory in Japan. After the War, the La Cloches returned to their home in St Helier Jersey in the Channel Islands.

Mum's eldest brother Willy (born October 1897, when Anna Rosa was 16-years-old), had been living before the war in Melbourne with his wife Muriel and sister-in-law Vivienne. Mum's youngest brother Bertie and wife Pearline, were also in Australia living in Sydney. The two brothers, both accountants, had retired before the war.

Willy and Bertie struck me as bright without having had the advantage of a tertiary education, and Bertie continued working in Sydney as a tax consultant.

His son John married Judith Anne Carton, a "Miss NSW", and had a successful business career before retiring at an early age to run a horse farm in NSW. Bertie lived in a Cremorne flat and I stayed with him briefly after graduating from St Louis in 1949.

I also saw him briefly in Sydney, before he died in the 1960s. Willy lived initially in Acland Street, St Kilda, and later in East Bentleigh, where he continued his hobbies of stamp collecting and carpentry. He drove an early model Holden and would often visit us at our Fordholm Road home in Hawthorn. He always brought gifts or sweets for the children, to whom he was very attached not having any children of his own. He was a kindly soft-spoken man with his head permanently cocked to one side because of a stiff neck. Our children loved his visits and found him an interesting old uncle.

One day I was called out of a meeting at work to take a phone call from Muriel who told me Willy had collapsed on the bathroom floor, and would I come to help him.

I found Willy motionless, having died.

Margaret and I subsequently helped Muriel and Vivienne with funeral and personal arrangements. We also were able to stop Muriel emptying Willy's store of whisky down the kitchen sink! Dear Willy left me his tools and clamps, his many cigarette tins and bottles full of screws and nails, as well as his extensive collection of stamps and first-day covers.

We continued to visit the two gentle and kind but somewhat timid and naïve sisters, until ICI sent us overseas in 1973.

6

Escape to Australia

Dad and his brother Joop were anxious to get their families out of Java to escape what they saw as the inevitable invasion by the Japanese, who had by then appeared to be unstoppable.

I remember accompanying Dad to the offices of several shipping companies to enquire about berths for my mother and I. We were finally successful one night at an office where I saw Dad handing over money, perhaps a bribe.

In any event this effort was rewarded as Dad and brother Joop secured two small officer cabins on a cattle boat called "Van Den Bosch". This ship had traded cattle between Soerabaya in Eastern Java and the island of Bali.

During our last days in Batavia, I asked my father to write something in an autograph book, which has a picture of the "Noordam" ship on its cover, or perhaps he asked me to do so. I don't remember.

This ship had brought us from San Francisco to Java in October 1941.

I still have this autograph book with his faded passport

photo pasted on a page and his strong handwriting, which I have ever since treasured.

My father wrote:

"Aan Pappie's lieve en eenige zoon, zoodat hy zich altyd Pappie zal herinneren en de vele uurtjes die hy met Pappie zamen doorbraght. Dat Ben braaf en flink opgroeit is de innige wensch van zyn liefhebbende vader. Signed J Lochtenberg, Batavia C., 20 Februari 1942."

His message translates:

"To Daddy's dearest and only son so that he will always remember his Dad and the many hours that he spent with his Dad. That Ben grows up to be honest and strong is the only wish of his loving father."

I remember going to Tanjung Priok, the harbour of Batavia now Jakarta, on the night of the 23 February, boarding a small cattle boat.

The ship when we boarded was already crowded, with many passengers huddled on the open deck with their belongings, which included suitcases, boxes and even some rolled up Persian rugs.

These passengers were to sleep on deck throughout the voyage as best they could, while the two Lochtenberg families made their way to only two officer's cabins as previously arranged by Dad and uncle Joop.

In these cabins, the six Lochtenbergs would enjoy some privacy. The harbour was being bombed by the Japanese as we boarded our ship that night, and my last memory of Dad was seeing him standing on the wharf in a soldier's uniform beside his brother Joop, with tears streaming down his face as we waved goodbye.

We pulled out of the harbour as bombs fell about us, and I awoke next morning as we sailed southwards through Sunda Strait between Java and Sumatra, passing the volcanic island of Krakatoa, which last erupted in 1883 killing some 30,000 people blanketing the world with a volcanic ash haze for several years. Java is an island with several active volcanoes, which of course intrigued me as a child, Dad once having taken me to visit a volcanic crater in the mountains south of Batavia.

Our cattle boat, captained by Adrianus Hofman was part of a convoy of several ships. After passing through Sunda Strait, our ship and a cable laying ship, which had a curiously bulbous cable-laying nose, left the convoy which headed west for India. Instead our two ships turned south for Australia and we watched the other ships disappear over the horizon.

We were to be the last convoy to leave Tanjung Priok, which was destroyed that night by the Japanese. We learned over the ship's radio later that several of the ships which we had left heading for India were sunk by the Japanese. The next ship to leave the harbour after us was captured by the Japanese and sent to Japan.

There was no explanation why our ship and one other separately headed for Australia. Perhaps the others had insufficient fuel to reach Australia or carried men or material needed by the Allies in India. If we had instead continued with the other ships to India and survived the voyage, my life would have taken a very different direction!

It was a tumultuous period then from our sailing date (February 23rd) to our arrival in Australia on March 5th 1942, a few days before my 11th birthday on the 10th.

Rabaul in New Britain had fallen on January 23rd and the Japanese invaded Sumatra on February 14th and Bali on the 17th. Singapore surrendered on February 15th and Darwin was bombed for the first time on February 19th.

In total Darwin was to be bombed sixty-six times.

At 7.00pm on February 28th, five days after Mum and I left Batavia, the "Perth" (a 6 inch cruiser) and the "Houston" (an 8 inch cruiser) sailed out of Tanjung Priok.

The Battle of the Java Sea which began on February 27th lasted three days, during which the Japanese lost four transports, and the Allies lost five cruisers and six destroyers including the Australian "Perth", the Dutch ships "De Ruyter" and "Java", the British "Exeter" and the United States "Houston".

The Batavia port had become a shambles with sunken ships in the harbour, damaged wharves with Dutch soldiers and civilians belatedly trying to crowd their families onto any boat. The two warships attempted to escape through Sunda Strait but were sunk 24 hours later by the Japanese invasion fleet heading for Java.

The Japanese landed in Java on February 29th six days after our escape, and captured Batavia on March 6th and landed in New Guinea on March 8th. General MacArthur evacuated Corrigador in the Philippines on March 9th and set up his Australian headquarters in Brisbane on March 17th. The Japanese thus made incredibly rapid advances in the three months following the bombing of Pearl Harbour on December 7th 1941.

So all in all we were extremely lucky that we were able to escape Java late in February. Dad's energy and determination in arranging our passage must have been stimulated by the family's earlier escape from Holland.

Everyone initially believed that the Japanese advance would be halted despite their early successes and this perhaps explains why my Uncle Joop, too old to be conscripted like my father, remained in Java with Dad to oppose the Japanese in the Civil Defence Force, although it is possible he may have been unable or unwilling to secure a passage for himself on the "Van Den Bosch" thereby deserting his brother.

The continuing Allied defeats and Japanese successes were unknown to the civilian population, but it was Basil Gotto, the RAF pilot boyfriend of my aunt Dorothy, who alerted my father and uncle Joop of the true situation and the rapid Japanese advance towards Singapore.

It is likely that Gotto reached Batavia on the "Empire Star" on February 12th, having left Singapore early that morning. The ship was badly damaged having survived three direct hits from Japanese bombers. The ship had been reserved for RAF personnel women and children, although a number of Australian nurses and soldiers were also on board.[19]

Meanwhile the "Van Den Bosch" was making slow but steady progress southwards through the Indian Ocean unaware of the continuing Allied defeats.

For a young boy on a strange crowded boat it was a great

---

19 'The Battle of Singapore', Peter Thompson, Portrait Books 2005.
   p 319, 321 & 322

adventure, and in any case I then believed that it would not be long before I would be reunited with my father.

In fact it was not until several months later in July 1942 that the Japanese advance in the Pacific was finally halted as a result of their naval defeat by the American fleet in Midway.

Unbeknown to me, I was never to see my father again.

Shipboard life became a repetitive but interesting routine. Every day another cow would be killed to make soup and stew for the many refugees on board.

We arrived after two weeks at sea, but to our surprise we docked at Bunbury and bypassed Perth. On entering the harbour we were astonished to see Bunbury's single wooden jetty crowded with townsfolk curious to see our arrival.

After some delay clearing formalities, which with hindsight were minimal, we walked into town with our few belongings. Our reception by the people of Bunbury was exceptionally welcoming and everyone was billeted with someone.

The two Lochtenberg families were put up at the Grand Central Hotel in the main street (now developed into offices), where we stayed for about two weeks. I remember clearly the generosity of many who accommodated and fed us. We were not charged for our hotel stay, and wherever we walked in the town we were greeted with smiles and offers of help.

The humanity shown to us in need was generous and widespread, in sharp contrast to the recent treatment of "illegal" refugees by the Australian Government.

After a short stay in Bunbury, my mother and I went by train to Perth and joined Aunt Corrie and her three boys sharing a house in Circe Circle, Nedlands. We next went to "St Louis", the Jesuit School in Claremont, as Dad had insisted Mum do whatever she could to provide me with a Jesuit education. The Rector at the time was Father Austin Kelly S.J., and he generously agreed that I could enrol on a no fee basis. This was something I have never forgotten in my continuing association with the Jesuits, and particularly in my relationship over sixty years with Fr Bill Dalton S.J. who in 1942 was a novice sports master at the school.

On reflection, Dalton became in a sense my surrogate father. My best friend at school was classmate John Sampson, who also lived in Circe Circle Nedlands. I had many meals at the Sampson home and Mrs Sampson was exceptionally kind to me during these early years in Australia.

The two Lochtenberg families lived together for a year in Perth, but Corrie then moved to Sydney where there was a large Dutch community and she enrolled her boys in the St Aloysius School.

Mum and I then joined Gran and Mum's sisters in Browne Avenue, Nedlands. However after some months Mum and I left this ménage of three aunts and grandmother, moving to Wilson Street and later to Wright Avenue, both in Swanbourne. The latter house faced a swamp (now filled in and developed) with the Perth Asylum on the skyline and Scotch College on a nearby hill. Both Wilson Street and Wright Avenue were near "St Louis" enabling me to ride my bike to school.

During my school days at St Louis, Mum found employment as a secretary at "Bouldens" – a lawn mowing and repair business on the corner of Stirling Highway in

Claremont, opposite Christ Church School. She needed to work as her quite generous Dutch Government Wartime Allowance of 40 pounds per month had to be repaid at the end of the War! As a result my mother's War widow's pension for four years after 1945 was reduced to £8 per month.

My first school year at St Louis was in Grade 6, which was the top class in the Junior School in a building near Stirling Highway, and known as 3rd Grammar.

It was quite a challenge to start Latin that year which I continued to study for the following six years. Study of Latin started with Caesar's invasion of Gaul and progressed through the works of Virgil, Ovid and Cicero. I achieved a good last year "Leaving" result by memorising a few of Ovid's poems and was very fortunate that I picked the one in the final exam!

An early forbidding figure in Grade 6 was the large novice master Mr Tracy SJ, who appeared to enjoy belting student's outstretched hands with a 15" heavy leather strap about two inches wide, often for the slightest misdemeanour. Some classmates received this treatment regularly, but I suffered this punishment only once or twice.

I graduated to the Senior School in 1943 and progressed through 2nd Grammar, 1st Grammar, 2nd Syntax ,1st Syntax, Poetry and Rhetoric in my final year. The teachers were generally outstanding, especially Fr Stormon for English and Mr Lobstein for German who was also head of the school cadets, although we made fun of the latter and Fr Perrott was Registrar and Fr Lawlor Prefect of Studies.

Sport was a regular afternoon fixture, but as I had minimal ball sense I never progressed beyond the football 2nd XVIII, or the cricket 2nd XI, both of which I achieved only in my last school year. This lack of ball sense influenced me to take up rowing when I entered University. What I lacked in ball sports I made up in reading, debating, singing and acting.

Having been weaned in my childhood on stories of "Puk and Muk" (the Dutch equivalent to Ginger Meggs), I progressed through the "William" books, then all the "Biggles" fighter ace stories, and finally all the John Buchan adventure books.

My singing included Gilbert and Sullivan's Buttercup in "HMS Pinafore", the Fairy Queen in "Iolanthe" and the Pirate King in the "Pirates of Penzance", all inspired by Fr Ryan. After "Pirates" my voice thankfully broke! My acting parts in school plays included Ariel in "The Tempest", and the male lead in "Le Bourgeois Gentilhomme", a play produced by Mr Lobstein which included the school Crock twins Gerry and Harry as gendarmes, and classmate John Eddy as the heroine.

At the end of my St Louis school days, Mum sent me on the interstate ship "Manoora" to Sydney as a reward for finishing Dux and Captain of the School. The former resulted only from my ability to achieve 100% in my maths subjects, thereby beating my brighter classmate John Eddy, who two years younger excelled and topped the State in Latin and Greek, where any mark over 90% was exceptional.

Eddy became a Jesuit and held Professorships at Georgetown in Washington and ANU in Canberra, where he died in 2011.

I was elected a Prefect but did not enjoy this role as the school was very disciplined under its Rector Austin Kelly S.J., who later became Australian Provincial of the Jesuits and subsequently in charge of the Jesuit Mission in

Bihar, India. Kelly required prefects to man the two school entrances every morning, to check that students were wearing their caps or summer straw boaters, that socks were pulled up and shoes clean! Prefects also supervised the distribution from a tray of one and a half slices of bread and jam at 5.00. Not very appetising, but by that time boarders were ravenous, and day boys who had played sport also joined the long queues in the playground. School food was meagre often consisting of saveloys and potatoes.

My last memory of Austin Kelly was when I visited him in the 1960s; he was a patient at the Caritas Hospice for the Dying in Kew, and had become a shadow of his former self. He was an extremely committed priest with old-fashioned views on discipline and deportment.

The best memory of my last school year was when I became School Captain, and a boarder, having lived earlier school years, initially with my Mother, Gran and Aunts in Nedlands, and then with my mother in Swanbourne.

With hindsight, this last year boarding helped me in my personal development. But the person who influenced me the most throughout these school years was undoubtedly the Jesuit sports master, Mr Bill Dalton.

Later he became "Master of Discipline" where his views on conduct were relaxed and differed sharply from the headmaster Fr. Kelly. He took a group of boys camping in the hills outside Perth, and another year on a camping and fishing trip to Bunbury.

I also remember him taking my friend John Sampson (who was school athletics champion) and I to the movies as a treat, although he later told me he was mortified when the film "A Town Like Alice" turned out to be a Japanese prisoner of war story, set in Malaysia and not about Alice Springs. I kept in touch with Bill Dalton through the years after leaving school, including when later he became Director of the Biblical Institute in Rome, and subsequently Director of the Biblical Institute in Jerusalem.

Bill wrote definitive books on St Paul and St Peter, and held strong views on hell ("nobody is in it") and also on the hierarchy of the Church, saying, "We need a Pope and Bishops elected by the Laity as occurred in the first four centuries, but the Church does not need the Curia!"

Bill would visit and stay with us in the United States, and through him my sons, Mark, Michael and Benedict were accepted by "Stonyhurst" boarding school in Lancashire when we lived in St Albans, England before we moved to the United States.

Bill wrote from Rome to Fr. Bossy S.J., the Headmaster of Stonyhurst stating, "You will be a right bastard if you do not accept the Lochtenberg boys who will be a credit to your waning establishment".

It was upsetting to see Bill near the end of his life, a patient with the Little Sisters of the Poor in Abbotsford, struggling and weak with a breathing problem, which had plagued him for several years. Bill died on Monday 10th May 2004 and I was fortunate that I was able to visit him two days before his death, although it was very upsetting.

At the end of my schooling in December 1948, I travelled on the "Manoora" to Sydney with Mrs Cullity and her daughter Margaret, whom I was attracted to, but alas my interest was not reciprocated. In Sydney I stayed with Uncle Bertie and his wife Pearline in their Cremorne flat. The flat was near the Cremorne Jetty, and although on my own I enjoyed ferry rides to the city and Manly beach. It was a relaxed and welcome break, before I returned to Perth to start University life.

Ben and his mother in Perth, 1943.

7

Engineering at the University of Western Australia

In 1949, Mum left her job at "Bouldens" to work in the University Accounts Department, having an aptitude with figures. I bought a new "Bantam BSA" 125 ccs motorbike, which then was an underpowered cheap two-stroke model, but it gave me independent transport.

My first challenge on entering university was to decide on a faculty. Fees were happily not a problem as the University of Western Australia was free, thanks to the Hackett and Gledden Bequests, and the University's ownership of the "West Australian" newspaper.

My first choice was medicine, but Mum backed by Gran, said the family could not afford to buy me a medical practice following graduation. I did not realise that I could have entered Government or Military Service as a medico,

Ben Lochtenberg

thereby overcoming this financial hurdle. As a result, I chose Engineering because of my aptitude in mathematics and science, and also because its practicality and logic appealed to me. I was not aware then of Sir John Monash's view that mathematics is the "alphabet of engineering".

In later years I came to recognise the benefit of a more general or legal education. The sole non-family advice I received from Jesuits at school was for a career in the diplomatic service, which as detailed later, did tempt me.

I plunged into my engineering course with energy and early success, winning the Surveying Prize and membership of the Engineers Club Committee in my second year.

The Engineering Faculty with some 250 students, which included ex-servicemen, was the largest in the University which then numbered about 2000 students in total.

Perth in 1949 had a population of 250,000 and the whole State of Western Australia including Perth totalled 500,000. Australia had a total population of about 8 million.

The strength of the engineering faculty led me to my election to the Guild of Undergraduates (the Student Council) in my third year, and I become President in my fifth year in 1953.

While a member of the Guild I met a cross-section of student leaders from other faculties, including John Stone (Council President in 1951) later to become Secretary of the Treasury, and Bob Hawke (Council President in 1952) later Prime Minister. Even in those student days Hawke claimed that he would become Prime Minister one day!

Rolf Harris at that time was editor of the University paper "The Pelican", to become later a well-known Television personality, but convicted of crimes in the 1970s and 1980s.

It is interesting to note that the Guild of Undergraduates or Students Union at my time was largely apolitical with political affiliations being generally a personal matter.

This is in contrast to student politics today which are a recognised SRC hothouse and breeding ground for Federal and State politicians such as Hawke, Costello, Abbott and Julia Gillard.

The Coalition's concern about student activism prompted the Howard Government's 2005 VSU legislation, which banned compulsory student union fees.

The total number of students at Australian universities has exploded over the last sixty years from 30,000 in the mid 1950's to nearly 1 million today.

A personal regret is that when I was Student President I was invited by the "International Student Service" to attend a meeting in Moscow. Mum would not allow me to accept this, being concerned that I might be detained in Russia, as the organisation was reportedly a communist front.

It would have been a very interesting visit.

My university days were very special and enjoyable filled with studies, student affairs and rowing most afternoons.

I also found time to join the University Dramatic Society and made an unsuccessful attempt to court an Arts student, Helen Maitland, who later married my predecessor as President of the Engineers Club, Peter Turpin.

Helen's father, a doctor, had a boat on the Swan River on which I was invited to sail on some weekends. I also accompanied the Maitland family one year for a holiday on Rottnest Island.

The Engineering School was a collegiate and stimulating with strong esprit-de-corps under the popular Dean Professor Blakeley.

The student body included a number of older ex-servicemen, some married, and one Garrick Agnew actually owned a car. The rest of us made do on motorbikes or bicycles. Professors I particularly remember were Prider, in Geology, lecturing a subject I enjoyed for three years, and Bayliss in Chemistry. I believed the Physics Professor Ross had passed his best years.

Prider was inspirational although he stated with conviction that oil and gas would never be found in the Cambrian Shield of Western Australia, being part of the oldest continent in the world. He was partially right in so far that when oil and gas were discovered later it was only offshore in sedimentary formations. And the red iron ore widespread in the North West and now a quarry for China was still to be recognised as a major minerals resource.

In my second year, I joined the University Boat Club and fell under the influence of the gentle and competent medico, Dr Pannell, and later more importantly, the outspoken head coach, Dr Gordon Barrett Hill, who was also a senior lecturer in Civil Engineering. A Rhodes Scholar with endless energy and drive but very short fuse, Gordon was to become a major influence on my life.

Rowing became my main interest and led to my close friendship with Ian Morison from a Doodlakine farm in the wheat belt. Ian was to become best man at our wedding in London. I rowed for several years with Ian in pairs, fours and eights, and after a shaky hesitant start, began to achieve success winning many races on the Swan River, and Intervarsity selection in my 1951 third year for the race in the Huon Valley Tasmania, 1952 at Murray Bridge South Australia, and 1953 in my 5th year Engineering, at Penrith on the Nepean river in NSW.

The latter is embedded in my memory as when leading in the three-mile race, I caught a "crab" near the finish, and we were beaten by a canvas by our arch rivals Melbourne University whose crew included Rod Carnegie and John Button.

The intervarsity races were major sporting events, preceded by rigorous daily training on the Swan River and Perth Regatta races before flying to the Eastern States.

It was a great experience to be part of a team welded together by the fiercely competitive Barrett-Hill, and there was no let up until after the big three-mile intervarsity race.

From Left to Right: Ian Morison, a rowing team mate,
Ben Lochtenberg and Gordon Barrett-Hill

We struggled throughout the year to raise money for travel and hotel accommodation, and always returned to Perth by rail to save costs. It was during one of these boozy return trips that the train broke down stranding us in the Nullabor desert for thirty-six hours before a relief steam engine arrived from Kalgoorlie. Unusually it rained briefly during our delay in the desert, so that the train corridor and compartments became covered in red mud brought in by our shoes. And more seriously the beer ran out!

My best memories of Perth University days, apart from rowing, were the periods of practical work experience.

At the end of my first year, I worked as a builder's labourer on the construction of new concrete piers for the narrows causeway over the Swan River. My job was to shovel sand away from the tracks used by arriving trucks tipping sand.

During the following summer of 1950/51, I was employed as a staff man assisting a Housing Commission surveyor. This again was simple work, holding a staff with regular markings steady while the surveyor looked through his "dumpy level".

Third year experience became much more interesting as Ian Morison and I went together to Tasmania for six months, to work for the Hydro Electric Commission on construction of a concrete dam at Butler's Gorge, and later an earth-fill dam at Liaweenie on the Great Lake.

Both sites are located in the highlands of Central Tasmania. While working there I learned to drive an HEC Land Rover, and more importantly to keep out of trouble when the Irish itinerant workers got drunk at night in our construction camp. Workers ate together in a large mess hall and slept in small individual cabins. Ian and I had one memorable long weekend break when we traversed the north coast, sleeping rough one night on the beach below the "Nut" at Stanley.

Third and fourth year engineering were each of two instead of three terms, and students were obliged to get approved six months experience in each of these years if they wished to advance to a three term fifth year and graduate.

My six months practical at the end of my Fourth Year was with the Aeronautical Research Laboratory at Fisherman's Bend in Melbourne. My first project was to measure the strain on the wing of a 'Mustang' fighter plane. This was held rigid at the body end of the wing, while the outer end of the wing was forced up and down repeatedly to simulate the movement of a wing in flight, when a plane is thrown up and down when flying through turbulence. Constant flexing of the structure leads to microscopic cracks, which become large enough for a break and ultimately total failure of the wing.

To measure the forces on the wing I glued small strain gauges to the wing surface and these were then connected by electrical leads to a recording device . This strain gauge knowledge was put to good use in my fifth year engineering research thesis. I used strain gauges on a steel wheat silo owned by the West Australian Wheat Board who had experienced problems with silo failures, as when a silo is filled with wheat, the wheat arches inside the silo resulting in a downward force on the outer shell, causing it to buckle if the shell is not strong enough.

I spent many days, measuring strain gauges, which I stuck on the outside of a Perth silo, while the operator filled and emptied the silo for me. By applying what I had learned about strain gauges at Fisherman's Bend, I was able to measure the internal forces of wheat on the silo wall for the first time and was awarded £100 by the West Australian Wheat Board, and this work incidentally led to my thesis gaining me an engineering degree with First Class Honours. A further tangible benefit was the £100 fee, as although that seems very little today, which in hindsight was a bargain for the Wheat Board, it enabled me to visit Margaret in Queensland but that's another story to be related later.

My second project in the six months at ARC in Melbourne was to have a profound impact on my Oxford degree and my later life, as it introduced me to mathematical 'Relaxation Theory'. Relaxation Theory is a technique used to solve mathematical problems which have too many unknowns, making them insoluble by normal algebraic methods. The technique is based on repeated minor adjustments to the unknowns which was laborious as my work predated the advent of computers.

This "relaxing" process is repeated until the residual discrepancy is trivial and the problem is then "solved".

The Relaxation problem I worked on at ARC was the initial design for the radio telescope to be built at Parkes NSW, which was featured in the movie "The Dish".

It had thirty-one unknowns in the algebraic equation. The figure of "31" has a strange connection with our family. Our eldest son Jan pointed out that our family number of two parents, seven married children and fifteen grandchildren totals thirty-one!

8

Meeting Margaret

Margaret and I were lucky and blessed that we ever met during the six months of my 4th year practical engineering, in Melbourne. Margaret was then completing her 3rd year of nursing at St Vincent's Hospital, in Melbourne.

I was staying in a boarding house in Kensington Road South Yarra run by "Bulli" Taylor, a retired Melbourne Grammar schoolmaster.

Most of the young men living there were ex Melbourne Grammarians and although I developed a friendship with some, my social life was focused on Newman College. This was because my school friends from St. Louis were studying medicine having moved to Melbourne University in their 4th year because Perth did not have a medical school at that time. Thus brothers Max and Dan Connor had taken up residence in Newman and I got to know other medical students including Noel Cullen and Frank Gorman.

Every Friday night, for six months, I would join this group to play cards in one of their College student bedrooms and join them socially on other occasions.

On a later September Friday, I arrived in Newman ready for my weekly game of cards only to find my friends dressed and ready to go to a dance. This was to be held at St Vincent's Hospital in the old "Out Patients" building near the corner of Victoria Parade and Nicholson Street. They explained that it was a dance they were going to and I had said, "I will see you next Friday" but they protested saying, "Come on, you will enjoy it."

"No way", I replied, "I won't know anyone there".

But they persisted and with nothing else to do that evening, I agreed to go.

The dance as I suspected turned out to be a boring evening for me in a room crowded with people I didn't know. But at about 11.30pm the night took on a very different complexion. Two white figures appeared in the doorway to the dance floor. Two nurses still in their uniforms having just completed their work in an operating theatre looked in on the revelries before heading for bed in the nurses' quarters above.

One nurse was Pat Gavan Duffy whom I knew from Perth as she had attended Loreto Nedlands and whom I had met at an inter-school dance. Next to Pat I saw a very attractive shorter nurse and I immediately thought I would go over and say hello to Pat and ask the unknown nurse for a dance. However I nearly stopped half way across the dance floor as I became aware of a man standing in the shadows behind the two figures. He turned out later to be Tom Spring, a Medical Resident at the hospital who married Pat later.

Fortunately I decided to press on; said hello to Pat, met

Tom, and then asked Margaret for the second last dance. After the dance, Margaret asked me for a cigarette, hoping to keep me for the last dance. Unhappily I couldn't oblige, not being a smoker. However when the band started up again we had the last dance and before we parted Margaret invited me to a musical evening at the hospital to be held the following week.

And the rest, of course, is history, although we would not have met if the operation Margaret had attended had lasted another thirty minutes or if she had not been working with Pat Spring, who I knew!

I felt excited and fortunate to have met this beautiful and interesting woman. During the next two months in Melbourne, we saw a lot of one another, although she had been going out regularly with someone else, who had a car and the resources to squire her regularly to dinners and nightclubs.

In contrast, our times together were much simpler events such as movies as well as one memorable day on a train trip to Frankston beach.

In November Marg completed her nursing at St Vincent's and returned by ship to Brisbane. My familiarity with ship departures enabled me to outwit her boyfriend who had filled her cabin with flowers. At the first blast of the ship's departure siren he scuttled down the gangplank, and I enjoyed standing beside Margaret on the deck until the later third warning blast.

I completed my six months engineering in Melbourne, playing cards at Newman and returning by train to Perth. I completed my 5th year, while Margaret was on the other side of Australia enrolled in a one-year midwifery course at the Brisbane Women's Hospital.

At the Intervarsity Regatta at Penrith that year, Margaret came down from Brisbane to cheer me on. Barrett-Hill later claimed that she had distracted me when we were narrowly beaten. The influence of Margaret's father, Dr John Lynch was already then evident as Margaret was only allowed to come to Penrith if accompanied by her older brother, John, as "chaperone"!

Margaret holding two babies
during her midwifery studies

It was Gordon Barrett-Hill who unexpectedly prompted me in my 5th year of engineering to consider applying for a Rhodes Scholarship.

The Rhodes Scholarships are world celebrated, and famous names abound among former scholars: Edwin Hubble (of telescope fame), Adam von Trott zu Solz (hanged for attempting to kill Hitler), Bob Hawke, Bill

Clinton (who left Oxford without a degree), and several Nobel Prize winning scientists and writers.

Not all the 7000 have found fame, but that was not the intention of Rhodes who, in his will, wanted scholars to be intelligent but not mere "bookworms", be involved in outdoor sports, and display qualities of leadership and unselfishness.

Born in 1853 in Natal South Africa, Rhodes at the age of 18 went to the diamond fields of Kimberley, and a short sixteen years later had become a towering figure in mining and finance.

During these years Rhodes attended Oxford for three years as an undergraduate, when he wrote his will which established his scholarships. His vision stipulated that the scholarships be restricted to applicants from the British Empire, the United States, South Africa, India and surprisingly Germany. Applicants had to be unmarried males, although that requirement has more recently been removed, and women now apply successfully.

In 2003 the Scholarships established the Mandela Rhodes Foundation, which brings some of Rhodes's De Beers riches back to the service of South Africa.

After initially hesitating to apply, I followed Gordon's advice and when awarded the scholarship, attended Brasenose College in Oxford from 1954 to 1956.

Gordon's mentorship was nearly my undoing, as he was an outspoken critic and opponent of the University's then Vice Chancellor, Stanley Prescott.

Prescott was also on the Rhodes Selection Committee, and attempted to thwart my chances by asking me at the interview to comment on any deficiencies and shortcomings I saw in the administration of the University. This was potentially an attack on his performance. I ducked his loaded question and after my leaving the room Prescott argued that, as I was unwilling to respond to his question, I was an unsuitable Rhodes Applicant.

Fortunately, the W.A. Governor Sir Charles Gairdner who was Chairman of the Selection Committee overruled him and I was awarded the scholarship.

Prescott had his revenge however by subsequently denying me the free passage to England, awarded each year to the West Australian Rhodes Scholar by the British-Australian Shipping Conference.

This led to me receiving £250 for my passage and expenses from ICI Australia and New Zealand Ltd. (or ICIANZ as it was then known), through the intervention of Dr Brian Smith, a Rhodes Scholar who was then ICIANZ Manager in Perth. Smith, on hearing of my plight, appealed to the personnel manager of ICIANZ in Melbourne, who was Dirk Zeidler.

The latter was to feature prominently in my later career when he became Company Chairman, but more of that later. So the Barrett-Hill/Currie feud led indirectly to my later employment with the ICI Group, although the £250 came with no strings attached as the Company simply wished me a successful future.

Such are the apparent random events and even setbacks which can change the future direction of one's life!

The year following my selection as a Rhodes Scholar continued in Perth. Having graduated from the University of Western Australia in December 1953 and awaiting my entry to Oxford in September 1954, I worked as an engineer in Kwinana.

Margaret joined me in Perth, living at Heidelberg Repatriation Hospital where she nursed. The Engineers Ball at year-end in Winthrop Hall with Margaret radiant in a blue evening dress is memorable, and it wasn't long before I plucked up my courage to ask her to marry me. I did this after visiting Gran and Aunt Eileen in Parkerville in the Darling Range, with both of us sitting in the open back of a utility returning to Perth.

Marg that night made an excited call to her parents in Brisbane, and heard from her sister Kath about her own engagement.

I spent nine months before Oxford working for M.W.Kellogg Inc. (now part of the Haliburton Group, which became notorious because of contracts in the Iraq war) as a construction engineer building a refinery for B.P. at Kwinana.

I reported to an excellent American boss, Bill Chapple, and spent much of my time keeping track of construction progress, which included climbing process columns each day to count the number of trays laid, or the number of pipes welded and installed in the furnaces to "crack" the crude oil. The site was near the old "Kwinana" wreck on a deserted beach, past smelly racks of hides on the road south of Fremantle. Today the area is heavily developed by industry.

Margaret and I planned initially to travel to England on the same ship to take up my Rhodes Scholarship, but Doctor Lynch objected saying Margaret had to follow me on a later ship.

We accepted this "advice" reluctantly and I departed on the Orontes leaving Margaret and Mum in Perth. Mum was very proud of my scholarship and this made my departure from home much easier.

Rhodes did not allow one to marry if you wished to retain the financial stipend of the Scholarship then 600 pound a year. So we continued being engaged until I completed my degree.

Life on the ship was enjoyable as I found myself part of a small group of young Perth graduates, all scholarship winners. The group included Geoff Bolton going to Balliol (later becoming Professor of History at ANU and now at University of WA), Barry Hammond (who tragically committed suicide on his return later to Perth) and Vic Maslen, the latter two both going to the University of London. Also in the group was the very attractive Beth McBride going to a scholarship at the Sorbonne in Paris.

I was surprised on the voyage to learn from McBride, whom I had been too nervous to approach at Perth University, that no one had ever asked her out.

The voyage lasted three weeks with stops in Colombo, Aden, Port Said and Marseilles. On arrival in Tilbury I was immersed immediately into rowing. I was met at dockside by three Brasenose oarsmen and driven to Henley-on-Thames to train for the "Stewards Fours".

Thanks to our coach Haig-Thomas (later to be coach of the two Oxford trial boats in 1955), we survived the early heats but were well beaten in the final at the Henley Regatta.

9

Life in Oxford

Coming to England in 1954 was stepping back into post-war Europe. It was the year when food rationing finally ended and people tore up their ration books. Only 8% of homes had a fridge and television was a new wonder. Britain was still a deeply class-ridden society, and Nancy Mitford published her prescriptive guide to the U and Non U in 1955.

Arriving in Brasenose I was greeted by the Head Scout at the College entrance and told that my rooms would be "Broadgates" in the New Quad.

This was built about 1800 as opposed to the College Old Quad, which was established in the 16th century. "Broadgates" was not on a staircase but was entered directly from the quad, and was next to the permanently closed College entrance to the High.

I had two large self-contained rooms, comprising a bedroom and a living room with a fireplace, as I was a senior post-graduate student. This was a plus but also a handicap, as I was not among other students who shared rooms on a staircase. Bathrooms were also a five minute walk outside the quad, which was quite a challenge come winter.

Soon after settling into my "Broadgates" rooms in the New Quod (now used as a College office), I hired a car and drove to Southampton, to meet Margaret arriving on the "Esperance Bay". I bought red fur lined boots for her as England was unseasonably blanketed with snow that year.

We drove first to London where we spent the night before going to Oxford. Margaret remembers us stopping at a pub en route to London, where she saw television for the first time. It was wonderful to be together again.

Margaret found lodgings in Oxford and went to work as a nurse at the Churchill Hospital in Oxford, while I settled into my research at the Engineering Laboratory on Woodstock Road. I had a false start to begin with as I had hoped to do my research in prestressed concrete, attracted by the slender bridge and structural designs possible with this material. However, Oxford had minimal facilities for concrete research, providing only such basics as shovels and buckets!

I visited London University renowned for research in concrete, but this was not a practical option for me with the Rhodes scholarship.

The Oxford Professor of Engineering, Sandy Thom, who was also a Fellow at Brasenose, suggested I make use of a wind tunnel, not in use at the Laboratory, or as an alternative do my research in "Relaxation Theory".

Thom was a recognised authority in both areas having led the Royal Aircraft Establishment in Farnborough during the war, and also being a world authority on Relaxation, although Professor Southwell had pipped him as the originator of the theory. Southwell had preceded Thom as Oxford's Engineering Professor, and had published his Relaxation findings only weeks before Thom did.

Another Rhodes Scholar from Queensland, Colin Apelt, was also seeking a research topic and Thom offered him the same options that he suggested to me. Colin and I finished tossing a coin, which fortunately, I won, selecting aerodynamics and the wind tunnel, leaving Colin with Relaxation Theory, which coincidentally I had worked with at the ARL in Melbourne.

It turned out to be the best coin toss I ever made.

Whereas I was able to complete my research and thesis in less than two years thus marrying Margaret in June 1956, Colin ran into trouble after two years work. Thom had forbidden Colin to contact his rival Southwell who had retired to a village outside Oxford. Unbeknown to Thom and Colin, Southwell had been working on the same Relaxation topic as Colin's research!

Southwell published his findings in 1956, and Colin had to make a fresh start and it was only in 1958 that he was able to obtain his doctorate.

My research topic was the transition from laminar to turbulent flow over an aerofoil, or aircraft wing, in the Engineering Laboratory wind tunnel. The problem I studied related to a de Havilland fighter plane which, occasionally under certain conditions, would lose lift and drop out of the sky. This happens when a "bubble" of separation at the leading edge of the wing, fails to reattach.

This results in sudden flow of turbulence over the wing and complete loss of lift for the plane, which then would drop like a stone.

I set out building an aerofoil with the same profile as the de Havilland wing using laminated wood, with help from the Engineering Laboratory workshop.

Once installed in the wind tunnel I had to become familiar with the tunnel's operation, studying airflow over the wing and recording laminar or turbulent flow on an electronic oscilloscope. I was fortunate the lab had a piece of such equipment which they had received recently as war reparations from Germany. This allowed several measurements of airflow at different wing locations to be recorded and studied at the same time.

Having bedded down and become familiar with my equipment in my 1st year, my next task was to reproduce the de Havilland bubble in the wind tunnel.

This took quite some time and I remember finally telling Margaret excitedly,

"I have found the bubble!"

She asked me, "What do you do now?"

To which I replied,

"I now have to find a way of getting rid of the bubble!"

This I managed in my 2nd year and I then had the challenge of writing my thesis, speculating on the mechanism by which air moving over a wing changes from laminar to turbulent flow.

During 1st year I rowed every afternoon after a special lunch provided for the crew at a hotel in Wallingford, as number three in one of Oxford's two trial eights.

The sixteen oarsmen vied for selection in the "Blue Boat" to race Cambridge on the Thames. The two trial crews included seven Australians of which five were finally selected (including Jim Gobbo, Jim McLeod and Vin Vine) and two who were to be in Oxford's second crew (known as the Isis Eight). These two were Rawdon Dalrymple, later to become Australia's ambassador in Washington and then Jakarta, and myself.

I also rowed No. 7 with Vin Vine as stroke in Brasenose's first crew and we earned a 'Bump Supper' in the college dining hall, having progressed four spaces (from 13th to 9th) in the Head of the River regatta at Oxford.

Some sixty crews in divisions of ten row in line (the Isis is too narrow for two crews to row abreast), where one tries to close the gap of two boat lengths between each boat.

The idea is to touch or "bump" the boat ahead before reaching the finishing line and before being "bumped" oneself by the boat behind.

Vin Vine (Front) Ben Lochtenberg (No. 7)
rowing on the Isis in Oxford

The regatta continues over four days, and if you manage to bump the boat ahead you move up one space for the race the following day. You keep your oar, if you earn a "bump Supper", which is suitably painted with Oxford and College crests and names of the crew and coach.

The "supper" is a major college event with formal dress, the high table in academic regalia, speeches and of course more food and wine than appropriate for any serious work the next day!

I also had the good fortune of being asked to coach the Jesus College first eight, and we went up four places earning a Bump Supper with myself as a College guest that night. The oars and racing shells those days were made of wood and much heavier than those used today made of carbon fibre.

Research work in my first year was usually early in the day or at night after dinner, because of rowing each afternoon. As a result I often worked until midnight. This work pattern could not continue if I was to produce my thesis and graduate in two years, so I gave up rowing in my second year.

Margaret also left Oxford in my 2nd year so that I would not be "distracted" and could devote myself fully to my research. Margaret began working as an agency midwife going to private homes around England, helping to deliver and settle newborn babies. We got together when we could, and I remember many happy reunions and sad farewells at Oxford's rail station.

Margaret would spend occassional weekend visits sleeping on a downstairs couch at 8 Polstead Road (off the Woodstock Road), which I rented in my 2nd year with two other Rhodes

Scholars Karl Lamb from California and Mike Garms from South Africa, and a golfing Blue Harvey Douglas also from South Africa.

Harvey's girlfriend Olga Deterding, who was heiress to the Shell fortune, would sometimes arrive at Polstead Road in her Lancia with her car boot full of champagne! Harvey also earned some notoriety, as one night he hit a golf ball from the New Quod at BNC over the Radcliffe Camera, which doubtless landed somewhere in All Souls College!

As part of my scholarship I had to meet the Warden of Rhodes House Bill Williams each term. He was an interesting character having been Montgomery's Chief of Staff during the war in the African campaign against Rommel. When Williams was asked after the war what he thought of Monty as a person, he dodged the question (or more accurately) dismissed it as irrelevant, remarking,

"Nice men don't win wars!"

I didn't hit it off with Williams as he thought I committed too much time rowing in my first year, and to engineering research in my 2nd final year. However my discomfort did not deflect me from my focus on completing my degree in order to marry Margaret. However I did miss rowing in my second year apart from rowing "Bumps" for Brasenose, and coaching Jesus College.

A favourite weekend pastime at Oxford was to scrounge a lift or ride a bike to the "Trout Inn" at Godstow, off the Woodstock Road roundabout. There we would sit alongside the weir on the upper reaches of the Isis River with a beer and sandwich on weekend afternoons. It was normal in those days to move out of college after one year as there was not enough accommodation in Brasenose for 300 students. However one was still obliged to attend College dinners at least twice a week.

My other memories are of going to the Oxford indoor market off High Street at lunchtime to get a slice of bread with dripping for two pence, or a bowl of fried rice in the evening for 15 pence at the Stowaway café on High Street. These meagre meals contrasting with formal college dining were a common feature of student life in Oxford.

A memorable event was when four of us from Brasenose walked from Oxford to London attempting to break Hilaire Belloc's record of 11 hours. Two of my flat mates Karl Lamb and Mike Garms, together with Brasenose student David Harrison (later to visit us in Melbourne as a correspondent of the London Times), arranged with the Café de Paris in Oxford, and a London restaurant of the same name, that they would give us a meal if we walked the 57 miles between the two cities faster than Belloc.

I don't know how Belloc achieved his record as Harrison the fittest and best of us finished in 14 hours. Of course we had not trained except on beer and pies! Only Harrison finished and I gave up with cramps after 35 miles.

The Café de Paris in London did us proud soon after our walk, providing a free dinner for us and our partners, including Margaret. It was a memorable night with Eartha Kitt singing, "I want to be evil" at our table wearing a slinky long black gown slit up one leg. Eartha was still singing at the Carlyle Hotel in New York in her late 70s!

Rhodes Scholars were also entertained while at Oxford by an organisation started by a group of ladies called 'The

Dominion Fellowship'. Initiated during the war, these ladies provided R & R to servicemen from the British Empire.

My first experience of the Dominion Fellowship was from Miss MacDonald of Sleat, who invited me to spend a week with her at Drumnodrochit on Loch Ness.

She was a sweet elderly lady living on her own except for a housekeeper, and who no doubt enjoyed an occasional visitor, even if only a student from Australia.

I was advised to bring a dinner suit and sure enough it was de riguer to dress up each night for dinner, after walks on the hills or along the nearby Loch.

It was a restful time with lots of reading and reflection on my career and my future with Margaret.

A sequel to this visit was an invitation the following Christmas in 1955, when Margaret joined me at a horse loving family in Cornwall. The family had three marriageable daughters and were a little put out when the Oxford student they invited asked if he could bring his fiancée! However they were gracious, if a little uppity, and recovered by inviting some young officer guardsmen from London.

The week was taken up with horse riding including a hunt which Marg and I followed briefly in a LandRover they provided. We decided to get "lost" so that we could have some time on our own.

In the summer of 1955 we were invited to visit my Aunt Dorothy and her husband Irwin Meyer who had rented a house in Hilterfingen on Lake Thun in Switzerland. We decided the best and most economical way of accepting this offer was to buy a second-hand Vespa scooter for £75, travelling through Belgium and Germany and returning through France.

The scooter was fitted with a wicker basket in front of the handlebars, which carried our food and a thermos, and a luggage rack at the back. A cushion strapped to this acted as a crude pillion seat for Margaret who sat in front of our minimal luggage.

We set off with great excitement from Oxford for the Channel ferry crossing after which we stayed in youth hostels in Europe. These were fairly basic except in Germany, and we became accustomed to separating after our evening meal going to respective men and women's dormitories. Margaret describes our Youth Hostel experiences in a letter to her parents at the time:

> "Bernard and I set off at 7am - we were held up at Tilbury waiting for the ferry to Gravesend and consequently missed the 2pm boat from Dover. Luckily we managed the next one - 4.30pm and arrived in Boulogne at 6.30pm after a very smooth crossing. Decided to stay there the night at the Y.H.A. and get away early the next day.
>
> The Youth Hostel was dirty - in fact quite filthy; but we were so tired we crawled into our respective sleeping sheets and off to sleep. Tuesday we got away about 9.30am - one of the rules of the hostels is that before leaving each one has some chores to do. This makes an early start quite impossible. I had nothing to do but Bernard had to sweep the boy's dormitory.
>
> We had a long drive, finally stopped for a picnic lunch

just before Lille - not very pleasant as some cows forced us out of the field - so on the road once more. We went through Lille and Charleroi, my bottom getting sorer at every mile. Anyway we pressed on to Namur and arrived at the Youth Hostel about 8.30pm. The Hostel was much better, and Ben was lucky enough to get a shower!

Wednesday was a bad day - after usual breakfast of rolls and coffee we both were given a huge pile of potatoes to peel, which again prevented an early start. The scenery here is beautiful - drove through Huy and the beautiful Meuse valley.

Then the rain came down, so we sheltered in an old farmhouse for several hours. About midday we set off once more for Malmedy, but going through the Ardennes we got lost several times. It was raining, and there we were riding up and down mountain tracks, getting wetter and no further along our route. An old woman we stopped to ask the way took us into her little mountain shack and made us coffee, and off we set again.

We only went a few yards and wet through we stopped at a lovely but isolated hotel in the Ardennes. It was then only about 3.00pm but we had both had enough. We had baths, dinner, 10 hours sleep, and after breakfast off we went again with lots of time to make up if we were to reach Hilterfingen on Friday night as planned.

The hotel was expensive, still we felt better for the rest. Thursday we drove through Blankenheim, Stethyle, crossed into Germany, a much better day but still quite cold. At Koblenz we sent a telegram to Dorothy (Ben's Aunt), telling her not to expect us until Sunday.

That night we spent at a YH in Boppard, a magnificent old home which had been turned into a youth hostel in Hitler's time. The YHA places in Germany are really first class - no baths or showers possible - but the whole place was beautifully clean. Were lucky here, had no chores to do so we set off at 8.30a the next morning."

The town of Boppard on the Rhine with the twin-towered church is indelibly fixed in our memories. We had no sooner left the Boppard youth hostel I was sounding my horn to warn two men walking in the middle of the cobbled street ahead of us. Margaret's letter describes what happened,

"Just outside Boppard we were driving along at the rate of 10 miles per hour - there were two men walking in front of us so we gave them a toot, intending to pass. One man stayed where he was, the other raced straight in front of the scooter and the next thing I knew, we knocked him down, bumped into a stone wall, and we both came off the bike! We picked ourselves up, got the old man onto his feet, no damage done but he said it was his last suit, wanted money, etc., took Ben's address and after he left we then looked at the bike. The front was all dented in, a thermos flask broken, milk everywhere, basket in the front all bent - but nothing serious."

Margaret suggested that we should report the incident to the police in case the old man reported us and since he had our address. With some difficulty we managed to locate a nearby police station, only to see the old man entering the front door as we approached.

"I told you he might report us" cried Margaret so we parked the scooter and hurried into the station.

In halting German/Dutch I explained what had happened and that the man we had knocked down had entered the station just ahead of us. The policeman behind the counter insisted despite our protests that no one had come in. At that point the man appeared through a back door and we shouted, "That's the man we knocked down!"

It turned out that the man was the cleaner employed at the station! The policeman after further enquiries fortunately said we had been in the right and asked if we wanted to make a claim against the man, which of course we didn't, so we left astonished at this coincidence. We also learned that the cleaner suffered from Parkinson's and hence his shaking.

Our next stop was Bingen where we stopped to buy bread rolls and wurst for lunch. We left the Rhine and travelled on to Mainz, Darmstadt, Heidelberg, Eberach and Lindach.

At Heilbronn the scooter started playing up, but we continued on the autobahn to Stuttgart where we got a puncture. We managed to get a lift with the scooter on the back of a German utility truck to a garage where a new tire and inner tube cost us £4. More trouble later with our spark plug, until finally the old Vespa engine finally gave up and refused to run. We realised then we had a serious problem.

We were outside a small village named Hechingen in

the Black Forest, and finally managed to find a motorbike repair shop. Incredibly this was owned by the then German TT motorbike champion who had befriended the then Australian champion. When he learned that we were Australians he agreed to repair the Vespa and that we need only pay the balance owing him on our return to England.

The repairs cost 130 marks or £13, and although we exchanged all our pounds, Swiss and French francs at the local bank we didn't have enough to pay the hotel and our new motorbike friend. If we had broken down anywhere else in Germany we would probably have had to leave the scooter and abort our trip.

It took two or three days to get the necessary spare parts, and as there was no youth hostel in the village we spent some of our meagre funds on a room in a local hostelry. The village that weekend was celebrating its 700 year anniversary. We spent the time with long countryside walks and a visit to the nearby Hohenzollern Castle.

We completed our journey to Hilterfingen through Schaffhausen and the Susten Pass, the latter at night waiting by the side of the road for a car so that we could follow its taillights for a few miles, as the Vespa lights had also failed!

We then repeated this operation awaiting the next car until finally someone realising our predicament took pity on us, driving slowly with us ahead in his headlights, proceeding down the rest of the pass into Switzerland. We were freezing and shared a brandy at the top of the pass, wearing all our clothes including our pyjamas.

Dot and Irwin when we reached them were gracious and generous hosts, and we enjoyed our stay with them before returning to England via Paris and unpleasant French youth hostels. Our Swiss trip despite all the scooter problems was a great experience.

Another trip to Europe at Easter in 1956 was to Uncle Joop, who had survived his POW experience in Java, and his wife Aunt Corrie living in The Hague, Holland. After our scooter experience we decided to hitchhike and did so through Belgium with minimal difficulty.

In fact we were extremely fortunate approaching Bruxelles to be picked up by a Belgian doctor. He took us to a lunch accompanied by several appertifes and later digestives, with the result that we were tipsy and giggling by the time he kindly dropped us outside Bruxelles, having said,

"You will never get a lift to Holland from the city centre."

Margaret waited on the road for a lift while I kept out of sight to improve our chances. Within minutes a large Mercedes pulled up. The driver was happy to take us, even after I showed myself. Amazingly he dropped us in The Hague, where we were able to board a tram for Wassenaar, where Joop and Corrie lived. Our warm welcome on arrival at the Lochtenbergs was surprising for Margaret. It was a very hot day and Joop immediately offered me a beer, but Margaret was offered a sickly yellow Advocaat, as it was not polite or the Dutch custom to offer women a beer!

The family was also somewhat agog that we were travelling together unmarried, and my older cousin 'Big Ben', then a doctor, was still waiting to marry his fiancée Maria having not yet saved enough to buy a house.

Margaret was also taken aback at dinner when Corrie peeled an apple for Joop, who asked,

"Would you like an apple Ben?" and when I said I would, he then asked Margaret to peel me one. To which Marg replied,

'He can peel one himself!'

We stayed with the Lochtenbergs during Lent when the Lochtenberg menu was "restricted" but this was not apparent to us. Meals were more than plentiful and on Easter Sunday the floodgates opened. Easter breakfast included a large bowl of coloured eggs, and the family each had 5 or 6 of these as well as slices of meat, cheese and bread.

The stay was a very happy one and we were taken to various sights and met other Lochtenberg family members.

It was one such occasion when Margaret was given the gold wedding ring of my Dutch grandmother, Dorothea, which Margaret gave me at our wedding.

Which, unhappily I have since lost in the surf at Broadbeach, having enlarged it because of my arthritis.

It was apparent that the family liked my father very much, and Margaret and I were the happy recipients of their affection and sympathy about Dad's untimely death as a POW.

I wanted to repaint the front fence of the Wassenaar house being grateful for our stay, but Joop was insistent that in Holland such tasks were for tradesmen and not family members. Joop had spent his working life in the tin business with the Company Billiton in Java and later England. During our visit we were included in a Dutch government dinner in his honour, at which he was awarded the Order of Orange, a Royal Dutch title, for his lifetime services. Joop established the International Tin Agreement in 1956, managing the world tin buffer stocks until his retirement.

Back in Oxford my viva, or in-person examination of my doctoral thesis, was set for the beginning of June 1956.

Writing of my thesis was itself a learning experience. When I presented the thesis first draft to Professor Thom for his comments, he suggested I read a passage that described a cow in unnecessary and clumsy terms, and how writing could be simplified and improved.

He told me to note this advice and rewrite my thesis. The thesis was examined by Professor Temple who was Oxford's Professor of Mathematics, as Thom being my advisor was ineligible, and no other Oxford don was familiar with aerodynamics. Accordingly an external second examiner was appointed, Professor P. R. Owen who held the chair in aerodynamics at Manchester University.

My viva began in the morning while Margaret lit candles and offered her prayers at a nearby church in St Giles.

I was cross-examined intensely by Owen and it became clear he was opposed to my views on laminar to turbulent transition, as these contradicted the theory he had developed and published earlier. After an hour and a half I was asked to leave the room, and following an anxious wait of some fifteen minutes in the corridor, I was called back.

Temple congratulated me and informed me that I would be awarded a Doctorate. This immediate announcement was unusual as normally one had to await formal notification about the outcome of one's viva.

I then found Margaret who had the forethought to buy a bottle of champagne and bring two glasses, and we celebrated the occasion sitting on a low brick fence outside the church in St Giles.

Another chapter had closed in my life, and we could now look forward to our forthcoming wedding in London on June 16th.I experienced a strange occurrence about this time, which to this day I believe happened to me.

One night coming back quite late from my work at the Engineering Laboratory, I believe I saw my father sitting on a low wall. He looked well and was smiling.

There was no conversation between us but I felt his love and support and in a strange way it made me happy and peaceful at this challenging period in my life.

Did I really see him or did I imagine it because of my need for his support? I shall never know, although at the time he appeared very real to me.

Oxford is a beautiful city despite the industrial section containing the original Morris-Cowley car factory now long closed. The university at its centre is magical, particularly when wandering its lanes on a foggy night.

The bookstore Blackwells on the "Broad" opposite the Sheldonian Theatre, where I received my degree, is where I first bought non technical books. These included "The Story of San Michele" by Axel Munthe, "The Republic of Plato" by Jowett and "Travels in Italy" by Abbe Du Paty published in 1788, which still remains my oldest book, predating later purchased "Cook's Voyages".

Our wedding day in 1956 came with a rush and there was barely enough time to make the necessary arrangements.

We had decided to get married in the Lady Chapel at Westminster Cathedral in London.

I don't recall why we chose this venue, but we were able to do so as Margaret left a suitcase in the Westminster flat of Rosemary Beresford (sister-in-law of Margaret's sister, Maureen), thereby establishing legal "residence" in the Cathedral diocese.

We had to attend a number of meetings with the Cathedral's officiating priest, and sent out our invitations to friends and relations for the morning ceremony. The marriage service was followed by a reception at the nearby Rembrandt Hotel close to Victoria Station.

Our only relatives able to attend were Uncle Joop and Aunt Corrie Lochtenberg who were living at that time in Chislehurst, Kent. Joop was then Chairman of the International Tin Council in London. Most of the wedding party was made up of students from Oxford with June English as Margaret's maid of honour, and my best man Ian Morison, then doing a town planning degree at the University of London.

Margaret's parents were unable to attend from Australia, but sent £250 to cover the wedding reception and our wedding present. We kept catering for the reception very basic, with Asti Spumanti instead of champagne and savoury snacks with a total cost of £43.00 (roughly $108 AUD as per the x2.5 exchange rate). The wedding cake was made at the Ashwell Bakery for £5, and an Ashwell friend made Margaret's wedding dress. Marg's headpiece, which held her veil, cost a pound, and her flower posy £5 from the Moisey Stevens florist in Berkeley Square (who are still located there). I picked a flower for my buttonhole surreptitiously from a house in the Square!

We were left with about £200 from the Lynch family cheque and with this bought a new pale blue Ford van. We chose a commercial van, which had no side windows, as it had sales tax only on the chassis and was therefore cheaper than a regular sedan. We proudly owned our first vehicle!

It was a wet London morning on June 16th but the weather couldn't dampen our excitement.

Ben and Margaret on their wedding day.

This was short-lived as following the morning reception we drove to Evesham in Gloucestershire to begin our honeymoon, having given up our earlier plans to go to Jersey's L'Horizon Hotel in St Brelade's Bay' because it was too expensive.

On arrival in Evesham I promptly fell ill for several days, as I was exhausted after the final weeks spent completing my thesis and preparing for my viva. Not a great marriage beginning for Margaret! Nor was our first night together very romantic, as having changed into pyjamas we learned there was no room service having arrived too late. I had to dress again to go downstairs and fetch champagne and our supper. This anticlimax was repeated a few days later after driving to Ashwell in Hertfordshire to stay in Maureen and Benedict's "Old Saddlery", the Beresfords then being in Nigeria. On our very first night there we were disturbed at about midnight, with a doorknock requesting Margaret to come and lay out a village friend of the Beresfords who had died!

We both started employment, following a week's break. Although our accommodation in Ashwell was free thanks to Maureen and Benedict, we were broke, as the Rhodes stipend of £600 per year had come to an end.

The scholarship had barely been sufficient to cover my Oxford expenses during the two years and I had earned some spare money working part time for ICI in London one summer, and as a casual mail sorter at the Oxford Post Office during the weeks preceding Christmas in 1955. The latter involved picking up any Christmas parcel from an accumulating pile and throwing this into a grid of country named openings. As there were several of us doing this it was easy to miss an opening labelled "Australia" and instead enter the adjacent opening "Austria". Unfortunately in the hectic pressure, it was rarely possible to retrieve and correct any error!

Newly married, Margaret went to work at the Maternity Hospital in Welwyn Garden City and I worked as a draughtsman on a drawing board at the Plastics Division of ICI PLC also located in WGC.

This was convenient as we were able to travel to work together in our new van.

I had earlier sought employment with de Havillands in Hatfield, as they had five wind tunnels and my research had involved their fighter plane problem. However they offered me a starting salary of only £5 per week, which was barely enough to live on. I made enquiries therefore at ICI's Plastics Division.

Being short of draughtsmen at the time, they offered me £8 per week, which of course was a huge improvement on De Havilland's offer. As a result I turned my back on aerodynamics, but I was also not really interested to continue working with wind tunnels. It had, after all, been a fallback research option for me having been unable to do research in prestressed concrete at Oxford.

Our days in Ashwell were very happy ones, as we were both earning a regular income and our weekends were free to travel about in our new Ford van.

We often went to London for evening plays or concerts, which sometimes meant having to leave the city in a "pea-soup" fog, while Margaret walked in front in the car headlights to indicate the edge of the road. London no longer burns coal for domestic heating so thick winter fogs are generally a thing of the past.

Margaret became worried after she started work at Welwyn Garden Hospital. She incorrectly answered a tax questionnaire about her employment history in England as a midwife, believing that now married the authorities would not connect the name Lynch with her newly married name of Lochtenberg. She became ill with this worry, so I fronted up at the local tax office, paid arrears owing and calm was restored at our Ashwell home.

My relationship with ICIANZ had not lain dormant during my time in Oxford. In the summer of 1955 I had obtained temporary employment in the ICI PLC engineering office located near Victoria Station in London.

During six weeks there I was given various assignments, including the design of an ecumenical chapel for ICI's Magadi Soda Ash Company in Kenya. I took great pleasure in some real work in the chapel design, with its sawtooth sidewalls with windows shining light on the chapel altar. I learned many years later from a visitor returning from Magadi that the chapel was in regular use and judged a success.

10

Joining ICIANZ in England

In the spring of 1956, I had a visit in Oxford from Donald Malcolmson who was representing ICIANZ in ICI's London office in Millbank.

Donald came with Len Weickhardt then Technical Director of ICIANZ. I was invited to an interview with the two over breakfast at "The Randolph", Oxford's leading hotel. This led soon after to a job offer from ICIANZ starting at £1,400 per year. After some correspondence it was agreed that I would start with a year's training as a "Work Study" officer in England, commencing in London on 1st September, before returning to Australia with our passage paid. Margaret and I discussed at some length this generous offer and decided finally that we would accept.

We would be returned to Australia after twelve months, and believed we would stay with ICIANZ and the chemical industry for perhaps three years.

Our short-term decision was to turn later into 37 years with the ICI Group! The earlier ICIANZ pre-Oxford £250 passage money to England "with no strings attached" was to lead to a lifetime industry career!

The acceptance of the 1956 ICIANZ offer had a good immediate outcome financially. When ICIANZ heard of my temporary job in Welwyn Garden as a draughtsman, they made up the difference between my £8 per week in July and August, and the £28 per week salary from 1st September in London, and late that summer we were suddenly affluent.

The time in Ashwell was really a working "honeymoon" of about two months in a delightful Hertfordshire village remote from highways and towns, with a rail-station located inconveniently some three miles outside the village.

Ashwell was the home of Maureen's mother-in-law, Janet Beresford, who lived at "Ashwell End" a charming pink house north of the village. We had got to know Janet through Maureen and Benedict, and had occasionally driven across England on our scooter from Oxford to stay weekends with Janet. The "Old Saddlery" in the village was Maureen and Benedict's English base while they lived in Nigeria for several years.

We moved to London in September to start my "Work Study" training, and rented a flat in Notting Hill for a month, which once again proved to be eventful on our first night. After we had gone to bed Marg said,

"I can hear someone moving about!"

I got up with some trepidation only to find a man settling into bed in another room. I asked, "Who are you and what are you doing here?"

He claimed the landlord had told him he could stay in our flat. I made it clear that was not the basis we had rented the property and that he would have to leave the next morning. Fortunately he did so without any further problem.

My start on September 1st as an ICIANZ secondee to ICI PLC as a trainee Work Study Officer began with a one-month training course in London run by a legendary ICI manager named Russel Currie.

Following this month of indoctrination we moved to Teeside Yorkshire where I was posted for six months as a naïve WSO with ICI's Agricultural Division in Billingham. My first assignment was in a workshop making steel drums to hold chemical fertiliser.

After a couple of days as I was standing with my stopwatch timing the operators, I was threatened by a tough burly operator saying,

"Watch out son, as these drum lids can fly off the machine and take your head off!"

I survived several months there and was then moved to the nitric acid plant night shift to study process layout for a planned expansion. This involved "Method Study" (Select, Record, Examine, Develop, Install and Maintain), the sequential "work study" steps used to analyse and solve problems, which I remember to this day.

Our domestic arrangements were haphazard which made it very difficult for Marg who was now pregnant.

We first rented a room in a house in Norton, where my bike, which I rode to work, was kept in the kitchen and hunted for more self-contained accommodation as far afield as Redcar and Whitby (Captain Cook's birthplace).

The bathroom in the Redcar cottage was in the kitchen where a hinged tabletop revealed a bathtub which could be filled with hot water from the stove!

We finally settled on a flat in Sands Hall, outside Sedgefield on the road to Durham. This was a stately home, which had seen better days, with a squash court in a separate building used as a chicken run!

Our kitchen was a small space under the staircase with power for a very small oven, which was drawn from a light socket. As a result, we often blew a fuse when we used too much power. However this was better accommodation and the months passed quickly, although Marg was often lonely.

It was here that she awakened her interest in antiques. At an auction she bought a set of antique balloon backed chairs. I reacted stupidly saying there was no way we could take these back to Australia at Company expense. Marg reluctantly exchanged the chairs with Mrs Laws, the owner of Sands Hall for a set of antique brass saucepans, which we still own, now sitting on our Welsh dresser.

At tee-side we became friendly with Ted and Margaret Challis, who as Work Study Manager, was my boss. We also got to know Bill and Tish Briggs, then a senior ICIANZ manager on secondment to ICI, and remained our friends living in nearby Caroline Street in South Yarra, until their recent deaths.

Our next posting was to ICI's General Chemicals Division in Lancashire, where we rented a house in Runcorn, after a short stay in the Blossoms Hotel in Chester. The house was a typical semi-detached villa that one sees everywhere in England, and which backed onto the local cemetery. Marg's eldest brother, John stayed with us and was visited by his then girlfriend, Mary Kelly, who later married Peter Thomson, the golfer.

John was with us when our first child, Jan, was born in the summer of 1957, at Liverpool Maternity Hospital.

John urged us not to rush when Marg's contractions started. This was nearly my undoing as the nearby transporter bridge (now replaced) was closed that day being Whitsunday. I had to drive the long way through Warrington to cross the Tees River. I needn't have panicked as poor Margaret had a difficult long labour. I bought Marg a handbag as a gift but this was stolen when the window of our van, parked outside the hospital, was smashed.

The trivial things one remembers on these momentous occasions.

My work-study jobs in Runcorn involved the carbide furnace which resembled Dante's inferno when the furnace was emptied of molten carbide into small rail trucks.

And later I worked on the rail system at Pilkington Sullivan works which I reached on my bike by crossing the rail bridge and riding along towpaths. On my first day I was instructed by the works manager to find some savings.

Two weeks later I proudly told him that we could save two cooper positions, as the factory had stopped making and using wooden barrels several years earlier.

He thanked me but told me to stop my savings study and instead direct my attention to the factory rail system. I learned later that the "coopers" were employed by the manager on his property!

My boss in Runcorn was the work-study manager John Schaeff, and we became friends with him and his wife Margaret. We also enjoyed the friendship of two colleagues in the work-study team, John Page Phillips and John Keith.

The former was a skilled rubber of old church brasses, getting permission to unscrew brasses and then rubbing the much earlier figures on the back. His wife Claudia astounded us as she had a swing in her kitchen suspended from the ceiling. Keith's hobby was collecting old pistols, about which he was very knowledgeable. These colleagues opened our eyes to new interests, and Marg herself became proficient in rubbing church brasses.

Our twelve months training finally drew to a close and although the year had been full of interest, we were keen to return to Australia. Now with newborn Jan, we were returning to Australia as a family. I had a large wooden box made by the ICI workshop for our meagre possessions, sold our van for £200 and headed off to Tilbury for the journey home on the old P&O liner S.S. Orontes.

11

Return to Australia

On reaching Melbourne in 1957, we stayed briefly at the now demolished Occidental Hotel in Collins Street.

We then moved to a rented house in Tower Hill Road in Nunawading, alongside a television tower just off Camberwell road.

The accommodation was fairly basic and we decided soon after our arrival to buy a second hand car. On hearing of this, Margaret's mother Kathleen said she didn't believe in used cars and offered to give us £1000 to buy a new one.

This unexpected offer overwhelmed us and after much discussion we decided to ask whether she would be upset if we spent the money on a block of land we had found in Jocelyn Court, Nunawading.

We were thrilled when Kathleen agreed and furthermore said she would lend us the money to build a house on our block. We then bought a house plan from "The Age" Small Homes Service for £10.

In what seemed no time we had a U-shaped unpainted timber home costing £3500, based on the loan from Kathleen for that amount and we agreed to repay her £300 a year. We were very happy that she wanted no interest on the principal.

It was a windfall gift, and I don't know how we would ever have got started without the help of Margaret's mother. Unfortunately the repayment agreement did not last long as our relationship soured, perhaps as a result of her separation from Dr. John Lynch.

Kathleen demanded immediate repayment of the outstanding loan amount. There was no way we could meet this demand and all I was able to agree with her was to increase the yearly repayments.

The new arrangement came to an end when Kathleen died in 1968, and Margaret's share of her estate was debited with the amount still outstanding, some £2900.

Marg used this reduced legacy to buy a flat for my mother in Armadale, as she had been living in rented accommodation following the difficult time when she had been living with us in Nunawading and then Hawthorn. We felt this was a good solution for Mum's accommodation, but she worried endlessly that she might become homeless if I should die, as the apartment was in Margaret's name.

Our Jocelyn Court home was very special to us being the first one we owned and where Anna, our second child, was born. We spent countless weekends painting the inside as well as outside, the latter initially forest green but later pink in memory of Janet Beresford's house in Ashwell, Hertfordshire, which we had enjoyed in our Oxford days. The Nunawading land was heavy clay with little topsoil, and it took many hours to break up the clay with a mattock and addition of lime.

The centre court inside the U shaped building was finally laid with concrete, and the house and garden was our pride and joy.

We initially bought a second-hand Austin A 40, which was later replaced with a new cream coloured Volkswagen as I progressed through ICIANZ.

As our overdraft with Bank of New South Wales showed no sign of reducing with the continuing expenses of improving our new home, I attempted to supplement my ICIANZ salary by enrolling as a tutor of mathematics at Newman College. I thought my earlier proficiency with maths would make this an easy source of added income.

However I was to be quickly disappointed, as despite preparing for the weekly tutorials, the sessions became an embarrassing burden eroding my confidence.

Among the group were always one or two very bright students, who were quick to draw attention to a simpler or more elegant mathematical solution to the one I was proposing. I was clearly rusty and I was relieved when the year ended and I did not offer to continue being a tutor at Newman.

12

ICIANZ

My first job with ICIANZ when we returned to Melbourne in 1957 was as a Work Study Officer in the Central Engineering Department (CED) which was then located in Latrobe street opposite the Flag Staff gardens.

The Chief Engineer was Eric Godfrey, who to me was a formidable Englishman.

My initial boss was Peter Saunders and my early complaints about working with Peter were not well received, although shortly thereafter I was moved to the Explosives factory in Deer Park as a development engineer reporting to the Works Manager Lu Donaldson.

I did not understand my good fortune that my outspoken and risky complaint was communicated to Archie Glenn who was a close friend of Donaldson, so it ended well for me.

The Explosives factory was some 20kms west of the city on Ballarat Road. It had been built in the mid 1880's well outside the city to supply mining explosives for the Victorian gold rush.

By 1958 Deer Park was surrounded by suburbia with

adjoining ICIANZ ammunition and vinyl coated "leather cloth" factories.

Donaldson was an inspiring leader with a strong team, which included Donald Malcolmson, who with Len Weickhardt had hired me in Oxford, being the Personnel and Production manager, and Ron Cherry heading technology. These were good days at Deer Park, travelling each day from Nunawading in a car pool with Jerry Wilson, Les Evans, Lu Schmidt and Ralph Sangster, all factory department managers.

I had a dread that there would be a nitro glycerine explosion with loss of life while I worked at Deer Park.

There had been a serious explosion a few years earlier at the N/G Hill, which left a huge crater where the building had once stood.

One never forgot the presence of N/G, as it had a sickly sweet smell and gave you a fierce headache. Old process operators were known to rub some N/G liquid inside the rim of their cloth caps, which after a time would make them insensitive to headaches!

The explosives mixing and cartridge rooms were separated by long safety distances, so that if one room did explode it would not propagate to adjoining rooms. Thus the factory covered a huge area, which involved a more direct hazard, as deadly tiger snakes were in the long grass between production rooms and storage magazines. Management thoughtfully provided long steel rods along the many paths that could be used if one sighted a snake!

The factory also included a black powder plant (the old gunpowder) where ingredients were mixed in a large cast iron dish, which regularly blew up.

This dangerous process was managed by making one wall of the building of very light construction so that in the event of dangerous explosions it could blow out facing Kororoit Creek, which ran along the factory boundary.

In 1959 I was plucked out of relative obscurity at Deer Park by Ted Kaiser, a senior project engineer in CED, and asked to accompany him on a three months engineering trip to Europe.

Ted was a devil, as although he was a tough and very experienced engineer, he had a keen eye for young attractive women as well as a great appreciation and love of music. He ran me ragged during our three months in England, Germany, Switzerland and Italy.

Typically after a long day visiting some engineering company, he would say, "Should we go to a concert or a nightclub tonight?"

And usually before I could reply, he would announce, "Let's do both!" At the end of such a night he would turn to me when finally we returned to our hotel at a late hour saying, "Ben, write up some notes on our meetings today."

It was an exciting and great learning experience for me in every sense, and I am grateful for many memorable highlights such as hearing Renata Tibaldi, in Vienna, singing "Tosca" with von Karajan conducting the Vienna Symphony Orchestra. But at the other extreme, having Margaret say to me a year later after asking me to take her to the "Panama Club" in London, "I am sure that topless chorus girl waved to you!" She was, of course, one of the girls Ted had invited to our table for champagne when the two of us had visited the club previously.

I learned also how Ted managed office politics, as when

the ICI Nobel Engineering Director Sem Wright insisted that his chief engineer should accompany us on a planned visit to Dusseldorf.

Ted disarmed Sem by stating that of course his man would join us, although I knew Ted was very much opposed to this. When Ted finally announced without any warning that we were leaving for Dusseldorf the next day, it was too late for Sem's engineer to join us!

The trip was very hard on Margaret who managed the family on her own in Melbourne for three months with two very young children Jan and Anna born in 1959, then aged 2 and 1.

We bought a second-hand TV to help fill the long nights I was away, and Kath and Brian McCarthy would sometimes visit Margaret, not yet having their own TV. This old set finally needed pliers to change channels after the knob broke!

Ted and I were hardly back when the Company decided to send me away again, this time to utilise the engineering information we had gained on our trip to design a new explosives factory with state of the art remote control as this was to ensure that operators would not be killed or injured in the event of an explosion. The factory was to be built at Bass Point, just south of Kiama on the NSW coast.

We were first to build a prototype "Mix-Pak" mixing and cartridge process to make nitroglycerine explosives at Ardeer in Scotland.

The engineering design was based on the best then available in Europe such as NAB in Sweden, Niepman in Germany, and Biazzi in Switzerland and Italy.

The ICIANZ Board thought we should accomplish this

project in six months, in which case our families would not accompany us to Scotland.

I will forever be grateful to Len Weickhardt then Technical Director of ICIANZ (and later to become Chancellor of the University of Melbourne), who argued that the task was likely to take longer than six months (In fact it took thirteen months!). Len won the day and as a result Margaret, Jan and Anna accompanied me to Scotland, and Ted brought his wife Muriel, leaving their only child Edward in Melbourne, as he was completing his university course.

We spent a little over a year during 1959-60 in Glasgow, living at 28 Upper Glenburn Road, Bearsden.

Mark was born during this time in 1960 in a small hospital in Dumbarton outside Glasgow. Mark's proxy godparents were Bob and Joyce Haslam who was then Personnel Manager of Nobel Division, also living in Bearsden. Bob was later to become Deputy Chairman of ICI in London, and after his retirement was made Lord Haslam by Margaret Thatcher for his work as chairman of British Coal and successfully fighting Arthur Scargill to settle the British coal strike in 1978.

Bob was very helpful to us during our difficult time in 1979 when we went to the United States instead of returning to Australia, and Margaret became a good, if distant, friend of Joyce Haslam. I count the Haslams as two of the really good people we met in our ICI career.

For the first six months away, Ted and I worked in the Nobel engineering department in Sauchiehall Street Glasgow, in what had formerly been the Beresford Hotel and famously a brothel used by American forces during the war. The building today is used to accommodate students at Glasgow University!

After six months Ted and I moved to Ardeer in Ayrshire, a one hour commute from Glasgow, to build and test our prototype "mix-pak" unit.

It was an exciting time from an engineering viewpoint, with visits to Niepmann in Gevelsberg, near Dusseldorf, which was a cigarette making machine factory owned by Gunther Moninghof.

We collaborated with Gunther to modify his technology to cartridge gelatine N/G explosives instead of cigarettes and this machine later became the worldwide standard used by ICI and other explosives manufacturers, replacing the earlier Dupont cartridge machine which extruded gelatine vertically into waxed paper cylinders.

Gunther had a beautiful blond young wife and I well remember her, for it was at a candle lit dinner at their home that I felt her hand stroking my thigh under the table! All this during dinner, while I looked across the table at Gunther, with the scar on his cheek gained in a university duel, prominently displayed in the soft candlelight.

At this time, we also made several visits to Dr Mario Biazzi, the world expert manufacturer of nitro glycerine plants at his factory in beautiful Vevey on Lake Geneva, Switzerland. Biazzi had developed his stainless steel fabricating skill as a supplier of equipment for the Swiss dairy industry.

In our visits to Vevey we stayed in a delightful hotel The Trois Couronnes on Lac Leman, previously a nunnery.

Biazzi also owned an explosives factory in Udine near Venice. My visit to Udine preceded Ted Kaiser's arrival. I was met by the factory manager who promptly took me to a tie shop, for which Udine is famous, and bought me a tie as a welcome to his city!

Margaret and Muriel Kayser later accompanied Ted and I on a visit to the original factory in Norway, where Alfred Nobel had discovered nitro glycerine in his home kitchen while blowing it up, and then to the NAB nitro glycerine works in Orebro, Sweden.

We sailed on this trip from Newcastle to Bergen across the rough North Sea on a ship appropriately nicknamed "the Vomiting Venus" - which was a trial for Marg who was five months pregnant with Mark! We had a cabin in 2nd Class whereas the Kaysers were in 1st Class.

We did not fare well in Norwegian restaurants with our Germanic names, as Muriel insisted on showing off her German which she had acquired in her student days when studying music in Vienna.

She seemed oblivious of the fact that the Norwegians with their World War memories hated the Germans.

Our Scandinavian trip ended with a delightful visit to Copenhagen and an evening at the Tivoli Gardens.

The 1960 visit to Scandinavia is well captured by Margaret in a journal she wrote at the time:

"Climbing from the grimy Newcastle dock onto the scrubbed, freshly painted Norwegian ship made us feel we were already in Scandinavia, and next day we were in Bergen. It was to be a hurried visit to Norway, Sweden and Denmark.

For once I was able to accompany my husband on a business trip. While he worked, I was driven around by wives of his associates and at night we were entertained in private homes.

The drive from Bergen, along the fiords to Oslo was magnificent and something I will never forget. Compared to many European countries, Norway is poor, but its people are happy and friendly and we felt welcome wherever we went.

Scandinavia is highly civilised, and has developed a contemporary style of its own which is simple, functional and beautiful. It affects their whole way of life – so different from us who still rely on the great styles of the past.

Art is encouraged everywhere. Typically, the two towers of the beautiful Town Hall have been turned into free flats for Norwegian artists. Our hotel in Oslo was delightful, its walls covered with ink drawings by their famous artist, Eduard Munch.

In all three capital cities, I visited their design centre, a permanent sales exhibition of contemporary applied art. I could go on and on about these places, the silverware, furniture, clothing, pottery and sculptures were magnificent and made me wish my bank account was not so meagre. Still it was a joy and inspiration just to look.

Vigaland Park was another place that impressed us, not so much because of the quality of the sculptures, but the overpowering numbers and size of them; 150 groups totalling nearly 1000 figures, culminating in a huge monolith 60 feet high.

Most of the homes we visited contained several original paintings and sculptures. We found the Swedish people more reserved – and their country rich and industrialised, as typified by their modern mosaic tiled underground railway.

During our two weeks the weather was perfect. The whole time I lived in cotton frocks and sandals. The lovely long summer evenings gave us time for sightseeing and leisurely dinners at open air restaurants. The Scandinavians' love of the sun and open air is almost a cult and we felt they spent every minute they could out of doors.

Religion doesn't seem to play a dominant part in their lives. One Sunday, Bernard and I were staying in Orebro, a large industrial town outside Stockholm. After several enquiries, we found the small and only Catholic Church, whose congregation consisted of two or three locals, ourselves, and the Italian band that played in a nightclub we visited the previous evening.

I had been holding my purse strings in Norway and Sweden, as I wanted to do my shopping in Denmark, and I couldn't have been more pleased with my patience. We found things cheaper and the people more helpful. I bought a beautiful teak dining table and chairs, which is now a constant reminder of our holiday.

Wonderful Copenhagen with narrow winding streets, lovely historic buildings, tall spires and fountains around the Town Hall square.

The Danes are fun-loving people. The Tivoli Gardens, modelled on the long extinct English Vauxhall Gardens, were crowded every evening. There were several open air concerts catering for all tastes, dance halls, dozens of eating places, expensive and otherwise, and a huge fun-fair. But what pleased us most was to see a mime. I believe the only remaining mime show in Europe.

With all the fireworks and coloured lights, it was truly a fairyland. The ship that carried us back from Esbjerg to Newcastle must have sensed our feelings at leaving Scandinavia, for its engines broke down in the North Sea. We wished it had done so long before leaving harbour."

Our time in Scotland passed quickly and it was a happy time because of the warm friendship of Glaswegians.

Only one episode marred our stay in Scotland.

Margaret was one day heading out to the airport to pick up a friend, with Jan, Anna and Mark in the back of our car, when she was hit broadside at an intersection.

Our small car was flipped on its side and the family was showered with broken window glass.

Someone in a nearby house came to help and then rang my office. I raced to the scene but could only see the upturned car, Margaret and the children having been taken into the house. Thankfully no one was injured, and this of course was before seat belts and air bags were introduced!

Margaret also made a special trip to London to visit her father who was staying with her brother John in London before we returned to Australia. Thus we had a full and hectic final year before returning to a more settled life at Jocelyn Court, Nunawading, in Melbourne.

After Scotland and a further spell at Deer Park as Works Engineer at the explosives and its adjoining ammunition factories making shotgun cartridges and 22 Rim Fire hunting bullets, I was moved to Victoria Parade in the city.

I was made Technical Manager of a newly created Building Products Division within the Company.

We were housed in a Victorian terraced house next to the St Vincent Maternity Hospital, which have since disappeared and replaced by the new highrise MLC building.

We were a small management group led by irascible Tom Mitchell, who was previously State Sales Manager for Victoria. My opposite number as Commercial Manager was Bob Geary who had transferred from Dulux, and the external field project manager was most impressive Bon Watson who had never got beyond secondary school but was an excellent executive. Mitchell bore down endlessly on Geary who in our second year could take this no more and resigned a broken man.

We attempted to promote and introduce new products in the market such as "Flexel", an electrical heating cloth which was never commercialised, and PVC pipe which was beginning to replace steel and copper pipe and guttering, now widely accepted and used.

It was a great learning experience and after two years resulted in my appointment as Marketing Manager of the

Nobel Explosives Division in ICI House Nicholson Street.

My new boss was Peter Demaine, a man of great integrity and ability, from whom I was to learn a great deal.

With hindsight, this was perhaps the most satisfying and enjoyable job in my long ICI career, not only did I have an excellent boss who delegated me a lot of responsibility but I had joined a great team who worked well together.

It included my earlier boss Lu Donaldson from Deer Park; Ron Cherry, the Technical Manager and Doug Shore, the Technical Services Manager who provided a bridge between the traditional rivals of marketing and production.

In this new role, I travelled extensively visiting mines throughout Australia as well as in New Zealand where we had explosives magazines at Waitawa and Fiji where Emperor Gold Mines was located.

These trips were often on my own. If the trip involved a technical element then Doug Shore would travel with me. It was on a visit to Mt Newman, in the Pilbara with Doug that our lives nearly came to an early end!

We were leaving the mine in a small Cessna, which taxied to the end of the runway before taking off. The pilot opened the throttle and with the engine roaring, before releasing the brakes to take off he suddenly slumped across the controls.

Doug and I sat there with the engines roaring and unable to get a response from the pilot. We finally got out of the plane and walked back to the terminal.

The pilot was dead having suffered a heart attack!

We thanked our good fortune that he had not died a minute later when we were airborne! As a result of this close call, the Company from that time would only allow employees to fly with two pilots.

On a happier note, my visits to mines were enjoyable and stimulating as mine managers and staff were always pleased to see visitors, especially those able to solve their problems, and we were always well looked after.

It was also a wonderful opportunity to see remote parts of Australia ranging from Mt Isa in Queensland, to Mt Lyell in Tasmania.

13

Visits to Japan

I benefited from very stimulating experiences during my four years of marketing explosives in annual visits to Japan.

To prepare for these visits I enrolled in a Japanese language course at Monash University and learned a little about the complexities of this tonic language (syllable emphasis being critical to meaning) and its two alphabets of 70 phonetic symbols as well as Chinese word symbol characters known as Kanji.

I began to appreciate the discipline of the Japanese mind when a 6-year-old is familiar with up to 90 symbols and several hundred-word characters, compared to an Australian child who knows perhaps 40 symbols at this age.

I always stayed in Tokyo at the Palace Hotel, alongside the moat around the Imperial Palace and it was a pleasure in the morning before work to walk in the quiet Palace gardens away from the noisy Tokyo streets.

My business meetings were challenging, although I developed good relationships with Aso-san from Sumitomo

Chemical, and the wily Kume-san, from the Mitsubishi group.

Negotiations were always protracted and a conclusion was only reached after a week of meetings when I announced that I was returning to Melbourne.

Evenings usually involved dinner at a Japanese restaurant with musical entertainment provided by Geishas, and generous amounts of hot or cold sake.

Many of my Japanese hosts became drunk after one or two drinks and they would have to be helped to taxis at the end of festivities by their junior colleagues.

On a less happy note, I remember one particularly difficult negotiation when the Japanese claimed I was lying and the tension became extremely intense.

I was usually accompanied only by an interpreter from the ICI Japan office, although my opposite numbers often spoke English and it was not unusual to have ten to twelve Japanese staff facing me across the table, some of whom would be substituted by newcomers during day long sessions.

Although these negotiations were never easy, they were very satisfying if I achieved my objectives.

Some principals such as Aso-san and Kume-san became good friends, and I hosted a celebratory dinner at the Melbourne Club with Kume-san and his colleagues many years later in the 1990's when I was Chairman of ICIANZ.

I particularly remember one manager Pierre Kuga-san, who during one evening's entertainment pulled out his wallet and showed me a photo of a young naval officer standing on the deck of a Japanese aircraft carrier.

"Me failed Kamikaze pilot" he confessed, telling me he

was fished out of the sea by a United States warship towards the end of the war, having missed his target!

Pierre explained his unusual Japanese first name. He had been born in Paris when his father was Japan's ambassador there. Despite the Japanese having killed my POW father, I never felt animosity towards them, recognising they were trapped in their disciplined Bushido culture.

Another memorable visit because it was so unusual was my business meeting with Madame Ohya who was Chairman of Teijin. She was a formidable and very rich woman, who reportedly owned part of the central business district of Osaka. To meet her I had to catch a train from Tokyo to a mountain town where she was living in one of her homes. Upon my arrival I was greeted by an assistant and told to wait in a reception room. After some time, the assistant returned to ask me my birth date. She left again returning later to say that Madame Ohya would now meet me, as the day and my birth were propitious! The Madame was elderly, large and imposing, and our meeting was attended by an interpreter and progressed well. I was able to leave after many cups of tea and the outline of the contract I had hoped for, details to be worked out by Teijin management. The episode brought me up against the history and culture of old Japan, and remains fresh in my memory.

During my visits to Japan, I attempted to see their martial arts and regretted that I was never able to make a visit during the Sumo wrestling season.

However I was successful in seeing Kendo at a Tokyo Police Academy, where police from throughout Japan were taught this art.

It was a very privileged visit arranged by Kume-San of Mitsubishi, at which I saw about 100 police trainees in a large gymnasium, who would yell as they brought their long sticks down on the heads of their opponents which were protected. Their intensive training included daily lessons in philosophy and psychology.

In 1969, I was sent on a three months management course to the Stanford University Business School in Palo Alto, outside San Francisco. This was a major burden for Margaret as I had already been away for three months in Europe with Ted Kaiser on the Bass Point explosives design.

The course included lectures and syndicate work continuing well into the night. We also had the benefit of visiting speakers such as Ehrlich, who had written a ground breaking book on the environment, and Malcolm X, the converted Islam leader of the Black Panther movement which was fighting for the rights of black Americans. The year 1969 was also when Martin Luther King was killed.

We were housed in Florence Moore Hall, a college housing female undergraduates during term time. I made a number of friendships there such as Peter Cazalet, who later became Deputy Chairman of British Petroleum in London.

During the mid-course break two of us hired a yellow convertible and drove to Yosemite National Park and then to Lake Tahoe, where we were ejected from the casino because we complained that we were not allowed into the featured Show, after seeing another group enter who were probably associated with management.

Several burly guards took us to the office of the "manager"

who looked as though he was a mafia member and he told the guards to throw us out which happened immediately through the Casino back door.

Margaret couldn't face another three months on her own, so with the help of the "Teams of Our Lady" looking after our six children, she spent the last week of the Stanford course with me. This was a "wives" week attending lectures and evening parties. The other thirty Stanford attendees were joined by their wives at company expense, with only two exceptions - One was a Nigerian who had four wives, and the other was myself as Dirk Zeidler considered this to be an unjustified perk!

As a result Margaret sold our Holden station wagon and with the proceeds bought a round the world air ticket, visiting Jerusalem which she had always wanted to see and where she stayed at the YMCA.

She then visited Maureen in England, where she stayed with Maureen's friend Margaret Collins in London who took her to see "Jesus Christ Superstar". Then followed Washington to visit the grave of her hero President John Kennedy's grave at Arlington cemetery, staying with a couple from "The Teams of Our Lady".

And finally arriving in Stanford.

It was a stimulating but lonely trip for Margaret, and it was good when she finally arrived in San Francisco tired, but excited for the final Stanford week.

We then travelled home together and were happy to be reunited with our children.

The "Teams of Our Lady" were established in France after the Second World War to develop spirituality and provide support for married couples.

We belonged to Team No. 2. Max and Stefanie Charlesworth had introduced the organisation to Australia as Team No. 1.

Our team was a close knit group and included our friends Frank and Kate Costigan, and Max and Frances Weston.

We had the benefit of a succession of chaplains including Michael Costigan (Frank's brother), Father Black, Father Peter Kelly (later to become Provincial of the Jesuits), and Father Frank Little (later Archbishop of Melbourne).

We were known as the "cosy" group as apart from sharing our experiences and life challenges at monthly meeting and discussing a topic, which included over several months, Pope John the 23rd's Encyclical "Humanae Vitae". We always followed mass with a meal washed down with plentiful wine!

Team meetings were held in turn at our homes, and also included occasional picnics, social evenings and weekend bottling parties. At the latter we would bottle a cask of wine as well as bottle tomato puree, having bought cases of ripe tomatoes at Victoria market.

The golden rule of "The Teams" was that you could always ask a favour, but it was accepted that you could also refuse a request. We thus helped one another as instanced in the Team's willingness to accept our children when Marg travelled to Stanford in San Francisco.

Anna Rosa Heytman's Home in Singapore.

A young Ben Lochtenberg at age 6.

Ben's father, Jan Lochtenberg. 1937.

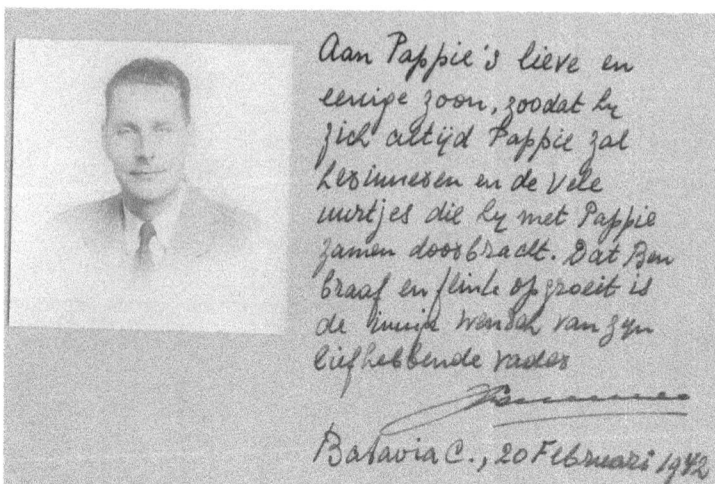

Aan Pappie's lieve en
eenige zoon, zoodat hij
zich altijd Pappie zal
herinneren en de vele
uurtjes die hij met Pappie
samen doorbracht. Dat Ben
braaf en flink opgroeit is
de huise wensch van zijn
liefhebbende vader

Batavia C., 20 Februari 1942

Jan Lochtenberg's message for his son.

Ben's father in New York. 1940.

Ben and Margaret at Oxford. 1955.

Margaret and Vespa. Europe 1955.

Pale blue Ford van. 1956

Ben Lochtenberg with his wife, Margaret and their children. 1991.
Left to Right: Maggie, Jan, Benedict, Anna, Michael, Lucy and Mark.

Ben Lochtenberg and his sons during their "Plus Four" trip to Hawaii. 1997.
Left to Right: Michael, Mark, Ben L, Benedict and Jan.

Trip to Italy with Margaret. 1997.
Left to Right: Lucy, Maggie and Anna.

14

Philippines & China visits
ICI England
1970-1979

I visited the Philippines in September 1970 as ICIANZ intended to establish a joint venture called "PEX", or Philippines Explosives Limited.

The President at that time was Ferdinand Marcos (1965 - 1986) and his wife Imelda. Both were to become famous for corruption and ostentatious living, especially Imelda who reportedly had a collection of 3000 pairs of shoes!

The corruption at the top cascaded through all layers of society, even into ICI's Philippines agents, Wise & Co.

I was confronted with this culture on my first morning in the Wise & Co. office when the Managing Director on my arrival opened the bar in his office and offered me a whisky at nine in the morning!

That night, the new Board members including this MD,

another Philippine businessman, Sem Wright (the Nobel Division Engineering Director) and I were invited by the Manila Chief of Police to an evening's entertainment at a new large Cinema Complex on the city waterfront.

I innocently thought we were to see some movie, but instead we were ushered into a plush small private screening room, and shown the first of probably several explicit erotic films. I suggest 'several' as Sem Wright and I stood up and excused ourselves from the official party after a few minutes of this 'entertainment'.

On the day between these two eye-opening episodes I went with Sem Wright by helicopter across Manilla Bay to the site for the future explosives facility of PEX and we were accompanied by a senior military officer as PEX was to be a joint venture with the military.

Although our explosives were solely for commercial purposes such as mining and quarrying, the Philippines government were very concerned about the security of explosives manufacturing, their use in later years by Moros terrorists was yet to happen.

Richard Woolcott, Australian Ambassador to the Philippines from 1978 until 1982, said the following about the country in his book "The Hot Seat" published in 2003:

"More than 400 years of Spanish rule, during which a fragmented and relatively uneducated people were exploited and Christianised (with the exception of the Muslim Separatist Moros in the South), followed by 45 years of United States materialist influence, had made a deep impact on the Philippines. Unlike the Indonesians, who had preserved their cultural identity

although ruled by the Dutch for many years, and unlike the Chinese who had absorbed successive waves of conquerors, any distinctive Philippine national identity had been largely submerged by Spanish and American influence. Filipinos generally were passive, patient, respectful of authority, and easily tempted by money."

In 1970 following Stanford, I was made Development Department manager, with a corner office on the 12th floor of ICI House.

I became a member of the General Managers committee led at that time by Henry Malycon. Religious affiliations were still important at the time, as I was reminded that the only other Catholic senior manager, before me had been Conroy, who was GM of the Alkali Chemicals group.

The promotion allowed me to park in the basement garage of ICI House on 1 Nicholson Street, and I was given a car and chose a Ford Fairlane. I chose a red model with white top but soon after this was called up to Dirk Zeidler's office on the Directors' 17th floor. I was admonished that ICIANZ senior managers did not drive red cars, and left his office somewhat chastened but I kept the Fairlane!

The Development Manager role was challenging and stimulating as I had responsibility for about twenty very bright technical staff covering a range of the Company's activities and assessing new opportunities.

We also used consultants such as McKinsey who examined how to grow our fertiliser business. The opening slide of their presentation to the Board to stunned surprise was "How to exit this Business".

Another project was to build a calcium carbide plant

in New Zealand. I knew about such a plant as I had work studied this operation with ICI in Runcorn in 1957.

We worked throughout the Christmas holidays and New Year on this project because of its high priority, but the plant was never built! This made me sceptical about "urgent" work!

I enjoyed my two years in this management role, which culminated in the "Redcliff" chemical complex in South Australia. This project was for a large petrochemical and plastics plant to be owned jointly by ICIANZ, AlCOA, B.F.Goodrich and Mitsubishi, the latter led by my friend from Mitsubishi, Kume-san.

The project was led by ICIANZ director Milton Bridgland, who later succeeded Zeidler as Managing Director. The project was a major one for the ICI group justifying a visit by John Harvey-Jones from the ICI board in London.

Harvey-Jones was a breath of fresh air and very different to the stiff more formal ICIANZ directors Zeidler, and Bridgland. Harvey-Jones was later to become chairman of ICI, but the "Redcliff" project was however never built.

I visited China in late 1972, during Mao's "Cultural Revolution". Chairman Mao Zedong launched his economic experiment known as the "Great Leap Forward" in 1957, when people left the fields to build backyard furnaces in which pots and pans were melted down to produce steel. The end product was generally unusable, but resulted in widespread famine from 1958 to 1962.

Mao followed this with the "Cultural Revolution" in 1966, which lasted until 1976 when Mao died.

In this proletarian revolution, Mao unleashed his rampaging "Red Guards" to attack and humiliate anyone considered to be an enemy of the revolution.

Scholars now believe that over a million were killed or driven to suicide and the lives of almost all urban residents were profoundly disrupted. Many schools and universities were closed. Educated people were forced to leave cities and work on farms, and as a result the Chinese economy almost collapsed.

As Marketing Manager of Explosives, I attended the Canton (now Kwang Chow) "Trade Fair", which was not what we know as a typical fair, but instead was held in a multi-storey office block containing a warren of offices.

In these offices during two weeks, one attended meetings, and if successful, negotiated a contract to import Chinese chemicals to Australia. The meetings were difficult and exhausting, and I particularly remember my opposing negotiator on the other side of the table to be a tough thin middle-aged woman from the Chinese Chemicals Ministry. These business negotiators were single minded and unresponsive to pressure, which made these sessions exhausting.

All Trade Fair attendees were accommodated at the "Tung Fang Hotel", a depressing large building, constructed by the Russians at an earlier time when the two countries were still friends.

However by the late 1960s relations had cooled and Russians were no longer to be seen in China.

Albania was the first country to recognise China as an independent country (as opposed to Generalissimo Chiang Kai-Shek's Taiwan) and was accorded special treatment in China as I was to find out.

Each morning after an unappetising breakfast at the hotel, attendees of whom there were more than a hundred, from Japan, Europe, Australia, Canada, and a few Americans as relations with the USA pre-Nixon were strained, would assemble outside the Hotel to await a fleet of buses to take us to the Trade Fair building.

On one morning there was only one bus, which was already crammed full and I just managed to clamber on, standing on the bus steps. After some twenty minutes, a Chinese official, recognisable because although everyone wore grey green or blue, officials wore shoes, approached the bus and said we had to get off as it was reserved for the Albanian delegation.

No one moved and he strode off, accompanied by some choice Australian expletives directed at the Albanians and Chinese. Another twenty minutes passed by which time no other buses had appeared and our shirts were soaked in the hot humid conditions. Finally the same official returned, stuck his head in the bus door, and in excellent English said, "I see, you must all be Albanians!"

Needless to say, we all vacated the bus, surprised at the official's humour.

My other memory of Canton is on one free afternoon, I decided to walk to the former Catholic Cathedral which I could see in the distance.

Canton was then a very low lying city, which apart from double and sometimes three storied restaurants (filled with families at night) and the odd taller building being used for the Trade Fair.

A depressing sight greeted me when I reached the Cathedral, which had been turned into the city refuse/recycling centre.

Trucks and carts would dump their contents in the forecourt, where workers would scour the rubbish for metal and salvageable material ,which was then carried into the Cathedral. I watched this scene for several minutes and finally plucked up courage to enter the nave and was surprised that no one stopped me. Both sides of the Nave were partitioned in about 3 metre sections, one with steel scrap, the next brass, then tin, glass, plastic, ceramics and so on, down the length of the Cathedral.

It was a hive of activity, and a sharp indication of the Government's attitude to religion and in this case Catholicism, which I confirmed by finding the foundation stone, which regrettably I did not record.

At that time, China was still ruled by Mao Zedong, a rigid authoritarian, who had come to power during "the Long March".

Mao virtually shut down China economically in the Cultural Revolution and many years had to pass before Deng Xiaoping opened it up to become the significant country and power it is today.

It was Napoleon who foretold of China,

"There lies a sleeping giant, let him sleep. For when he wakes, he will move the world."

I was impressed by the cleanliness and regimentation of China compared with Hong Kong, despite the blaring martial music and posters in every major street. I bought two green Mao jackets and caps for our young sons Michael and Benedict.

In 1973, I was seconded to ICI Plastics Division in England. My agreement to move to the position in England was not welcomed by my then boss, Milton Bridgland, who bluntly told me, "You will not be worth two bob on your return if you go to England!"

Margaret and I had no way of knowing at the time that we would be away from Australia for twenty years!

The secondment to England was to be for only three years. I went to the Women's Maternity Hospital in Carlton to break the news to Margaret who was there awaiting the caesarian birth of Lucy our seventh child, and was fortunately lying down.

She took the news remarkably well as we both saw the move as an exciting opportunity for the family as well as my career. Our only disappointment was to leave our home in Fordholm Road, Hawthorn. We had lived there for over ten years, converting the wreck we had bought into an attractive home with a pool in the back garden. We had moved from Jocelyn Court where with our growing family of three young children, we were bursting at the seams. Mum had joined us and lived in the dining room, which we converted into her bedroom.

Our search for a larger home had proved difficult on my income, and with the equity in Jocelyn Court burdened with the loan from Margaret's mother, only extinguished later at her death. We finally settled on a run down Edwardian house in Fordholm road, built in 1917. The AMP and banks would not give us a mortgage on the property, which they regarded as a ruin deserving to be pulled down!

Thankfully ICIANZ finally agreed to guarantee a loan with the Bank of New South Wales (now Westpac).

We bought the house for £10,750 and moved in the

night Michael was born on 12th May 1962. Our new home absorbed our weekends during the following years, with Margaret and I initially rubbing the old layers of calsomine off the walls, revealing bare plaster, before painting or wallpapering.

We continued slowly to make improvements, with my mother living in an upstairs back bedroom, and taking a lodger, Miss Lands, who lived downstairs in what later became our dining room, when my income improved.

It was a busy and very happy family time with births of Michael in 1962, our fifth child Benedict in 1963, and a second daughter and sixth child Margaret Mary, known as 'Bubs', in 1965.

We added a pool and patio in the back garden.

To help finance the pool, Marg enrolled in a nursing refresher course and worked night duty at the Heidelberg Repatriation Hospital. She followed this later with night duty at the Maternity Women Hospital's annexe in Studley Park Road, now part of Burke Hall School.

The pool was still incomplete when Marg had to give up her nursing job as she became pregnant with Lucy who was born in April 1973.

Our home was extremely well located for schools and tramlines. Anna attended the Brigidene Convent at the end of Fordholm Road. Mark, followed later by Michael and Benedict, went to St Johns school nearby on Glenferrie Road which was run by the Marist Brothers. Margaret Mary went to Manresa kindergarten behind the church of the Immaculate Conception on Glenferrie Road, and Jan attended Burke Hall and later Xavier.

One memory of our home in Hawthorn was a night when I was overseas. Margaret saw a huntsman spider in our bedroom when retiring to bed. Alarmed she went out on Fordholm Road and accosted a man walking his dog, asking him to enter the house to kill the spider. Happily he agreed to do this, no doubt with some trepidation!

We left our home for England in September 1973, having just laid new carpets and were enjoying our wonderful location, outdoor courtyard and pool.

Many of our friends from "The Teams" came to Tullamarine to farewell us and our seven children, who were ranging from Jan at age 16 to the newborn Lucy, all of us travelling luxuriously in first class courtesy of ICI.

The journey was quite an expedition flying on a QANTAS 707 with stops in Hong Kong and Athens en route to London. The stop in Hong Kong was magical as we stayed at the Peninsula Hotel, with two of their Rolls Royce cars meeting our large family at the airport. We were entertained the next day by the local ICI manager John Chandler and his Chilean wife Peky, sailing on the harbour on an ICI owned Chinese junk. At our next stop in Athens we stayed at a hotel at Glyfada near the airport, and found time to hire a VW van to visit the Acropolis, and temple ruins at Sounion.

We experienced a hiccup when we arrived at London's Heathrow airport, as Jan and Mark were allowed immediate entry because of their British births, but the rest of us were delayed as we had been issued with inappropriate visas by the British High Commission in Australia. Though we were finally allowed to enter after a delay of some hours when an ICI personnel manager arrived to vouch for us.

The trip from Melbourne to London, with two stopovers, had taken a week, and we were happy to arrive at the 'Moat House' hotel in Harpenden, Hertfordshire. We stayed at the hotel for several weeks until we were able to rent a house.

It was a hectic time settling Jan and Mark into St Alban's Grammar, Anna into Loreto, Michael into St Albans Comprehensive school, and Benedict and Maggie into St Albans and Stephens primary.

Meantime, I was thrown into the deep end as Commercial Services and Overseas director, not knowing that the Plastics Division Chairman Charles Vowles had been pressured to accept me! My arrival precipitated the early retirement of my predecessor Henry Raine.

Henry died tragically shortly after my arrival in a car accident.

The first home we rented was in Cunningham Hill Road in St Albans just off the main road to London, owned by Norman McLeod. Previously a Plastics Division deputy chairman, McLeod had gone to Tokyo as MD of ICI Japan.

It was a characterless house and we bought furniture for it at Welwyn Garden. But we have good memories of our children playing together in the back garden, and sitting by the fire reading Sunday papers on winter days.

I initially found work a struggle and soon confessed to Margaret that I feared I would fail.

The Plastics board then was large numbering twelve directors, and although I tried to contribute to board discussions, I felt I was being ignored. However, after some time, I learned to modify my direct Australian approach having observed the English way. The others would begin their comments by agreeing with the proposition being discussed, but then gently introduce their criticisms.

This approach, which I then developed successfully, was disastrous when I applied it later when I was transferred to the United States, as I will detail later. Thus with time and studied tact, my contributions became accepted and my confidence grew.

After a year my responsibilities were changed to speciality plastics such as acrylic "Perspex" and "Fluon" which was ICI's equivalent to DuPont's "Teflon". This area was more interesting than my initial purchasing and distribution role and involved visits to DuPont and Union Carbide in the United States.

I was also at that time put on the ICI Holland board known as the Raad van Commissarissen, which met monthly at ICI's Rozenburg site near Rotterdam.

To recover my Dutch, I was enrolled in a language school in Scheveningen. I enjoyed becoming familiar again with my childhood language, although technical discussions at board meetings continued to confound me.

However I met several interesting and stimulating people during my visits to Holland.

After completing three years with ICI's Plastics division we were due to return to Australia. But this did not eventuate as Zeidler, ICI Australia's Chairman, said there was no appropriate position for me in Melbourne. Instead I was given a new responsibility at Plastics Division as Director in charge of "Films", which involved "Melinex" polyester film (with factories in Scotland, Holland and the

USA), "Propafilm" polypropylene film (with factories in Scotland and Belgium), "Visqueen" polyethelene film and "Bexford" photographic film, both produced in England.

This interesting new job was to occupy me for the next three years and involved extensive travel and interaction with other film producers such as BASF and Hoechst in Germany, Mont Edison in Italy, and Dupont and Mobil in the United States.

15

Visits to Russia

1975 & 1978

My first visit to Russia in 1975 resulted from an invitation to give a speech to the Russian Academy of Science, on high performance plastics such as "PES" (Polyether Sulphate), "FLUON" and "Acrylics" which is an older plastic first used in the Second World War for fighter plane canopies, and now used for car tail lights.

I had always wanted to visit Russia and was sorry not to have done so in 1953 when I was invited to Moscow when President of the University of Western Australia's Guild of Undergraduates. At that time East-West relationships were tense and Mum urged me to refuse the invitation, which in youthful obedience I did reluctantly!

So the 1975 visit almost a generation later was a thrill if rather a bleak experience. The lecture I gave through a translator, was a non-event, but the following dinner with the Academy was memorable, except that I had to return endless number of toasts to Russia, the President, Great Britain, the Queen, the Academy, ICI PLC, etc. etc.

I struggled to remain sober through the very long dinner.

My hotel, the Moscova, provided unappetising food in the dining room, and I have memories of the nearby main thoroughfare Gorky Avenue where a centre lane was reserved for sole use of the Politburo, and the magnificent Moscow Subway whose stations were decorated with statues and marble.

Changing of the guard by three soldiers at midnight outside Lenin's tomb near the Kremlin raised the hairs on my neck, their boots ringing on the cobbled road.

My only entry to the Kremlin was to see the Bolshoi Ballet's magic thanks to ICI's trading agent in Moscow, having failed to buy a ticket at the hotel. Earlier at the Moscova I made a reservation and paid for a Bolshoi ticket but was told to collect this on the morning of the performance. When I later attempted to collect my ticket I was told I had no reservation.

Angrily I grabbed the reservation book from the clerk, turned back a page or two and pointed out my name showing the amount I had paid. Unperturbed, the clerk said there must have been a mistake and returned the ticket money to me. My anger was wasted on the clerk, but fortunately ICI's agent was able to get me a seat, no doubt with payment of some roubles.

I was enthralled with the tall willowy prima ballerina, and believe her name was Maximova, dancing as "Giselle".

My other memory of the Moscova Hotel was that there were no telephone books in 1975.

To make a call, you had to go to a special desk in the lobby where a clerk had an exercise book containing handwritten Moscow numbers, and she would book you a call – no doubt a Government means of keeping track of calls made by visitors.

I discovered another example of surveillance in my bedroom. I had been warned that if I wished to have a private conversation I should do so in my adjoining bathroom with the tap running.

This warning was confirmed when I checked out of the Hotel. As I was getting into a taxi to take me to the airport, I remembered that I had left my coat in the bedroom cupboard. On my return to my bedroom, my surprise was matched by a lady standing on a short ladder in the centre of the room, she was cleaning or adjusting a small microphone, which was hanging from the bedroom light fitting!

On arrival at Moscow airport, my bag was screened as it had been on arrival. When the British Airways plane finally took off, there was spontaneous cheering and clapping from passengers, pleased to be leaving this "Workers' Paradise"!

My second visit to Russia in 1978 was to officially open the "Melinex" polyester film facility which ICI had licensed to Russia.

The ICI Chairman at the time, John Harvey-Jones, was a great believer in licensing the Russians although the United States and many other countries opposed such technology transfers. John believed that anything we could do to lift Russian standard of living would be to the long-term detriment of Communism.

ICI had over 100 technicians and family members based in Vladimir, the historical capital of Russia, some 250 miles east of Moscow on the main highway east to Siberia. Vladimir was the centre of the Russian plastics industry and also where Gary Powers was incarcerated.

Powers was the United States Air Force pilot of the U2 high flying reconnaissance aircraft which was shot down over Sverdlovsk, Siberia in 1960. This incident was a propaganda coup for Nikita Kruschev and led to the cancellation of a planned visit to Russia by Dwight Eisenhower, then US President.

We travelled from Moscow to Vladimir by car and were stopped about every fifty miles by a security checkpoint to inspect the car and our papers. In Vladimir, I was accommodated in a high-rise building, which housed the ICI families.

During my visit I met with the wives, and distributed packets of porridge oats as well as chocolates, which were not procurable in Russia. Most of the ICI team were Scottish from Dumfries where ICI had its main 'Melinex' operations. The wives had a desperate time during the 18 months to two years they were in Russia and tragically one wife committed suicide as a result of the harsh conditions.

I was appalled with the attitude and morale of the Russian plant operators. Although all the critical control and electronic equipment was imported from ICI in Scotland, installation was very poor resulting in continuing malfunctions and these were only rectified when a special team from the military was brought in. These white coated specialists were part of Russia's technical elite, indicating the priority Russia gave to defence and the military.

My farewell lunch with the Russian manager of the

Vladimir Plastics Factory was an eye-opener. I asked him if he was unwell as he looked poorly. He replied that he always tried to appear unwell at that particular time of the year, as his state of health provided points towards his holiday entitlement each year. He also earned points if he attained the factory production quota and also if the factory political commissar judged that he had the right "attitude" to the workers.

Perhaps the last factor is why I had seen stretchers behind the operating control panels, allowing shift operators to sleep during the night!

The Manager went on to say that if his points total was sufficiently high, he would qualify for a holiday on the Black Sea, whereas if his total was low, he merited only a holiday in a local "boarding house". The manager's wife was a doctor and usually earned a different point total to his, and it had been two or three years since they had enjoyed a holiday together! All this was revealed to me by a senior communist party 'apparatchik' responsible for the largest plastics factory in Russia.

The high-rise building that accommodated me had lifts but these didn't operate every day and when I complained to the Building Commissar, a feisty elderly woman, that my bathtub which had no shower, did not have a bath plug, she said that Russians refused to sit in dirty bath water the way Westerners would. This land of the glorious revolution!

Muscovites who were senior enough to own a car usually removed their windscreen wipers when they parked in the city, to avoid having them stolen.

Conditions in Russia of course are vastly improved today

since the Berlin Wall fell in 1989, leading to the collapse of the Soviet Union. The principal actor in this climactic development was Mikhail Gorbachev who in speeches he made in 1988 completely misjudged the people's pent-up yearning for access to commodities, luxury goods and services. In Gorbachev's last years of leadership, wages and pensions went unpaid and even battery hens died from lack of feed.

During our time at Plastics Division we became friendly with Sandy Thom, then Deputy Chairman, and his wife Anne. They invited us to sail on their boat out of Chicester and also join them for a ski holiday at Mottaret, in the Trois Vallees. The latter became quite a challenge as evenings would start with whisky, and dinner cooked by Anne would not be served until 9.30pm. By then we were "away with the birds" and had lost our appetite. Marg's offer to cook the evening meal was rebuffed, and so we suffered throughout the week.

Sandy Thom was also later the reason for a late night row I had with Margaret at the Savoy Hotel on the Strand.

The legendary Art Deco Savoy which opened in 1889, was London's first luxury hotel built by the theatre impresario D'Oyly Carte. Each year Plastics Division hosted a dinner at the Savoy, called the "PIGS" Night (Plastics Industry Golf Society). Thom was the regular host but that year he fell ill and I became the substitute host, so that Margaret and I occupied a magnificent riverside suite.

After a very late dinner which included dancing, our business guests joined us in our rooms and drinks flowed freely until late in the night. Margaret finally went to bed and asked me to get rid of our increasingly noisy guests in the adjoining rooms. I said this was not possible as they were our best customers, and this did not go down well!

The Plastics Board would hold one meeting each year off site somewhere in Europe, and the visit to Italy was a highlight when we stayed at the Villa d'Este on Lake Como. Marg and I had a room with balcony overlooking the lake, which took our breath away on the moonlit nights.

A final comment is appropriate about the stratified ICI conditions at Welwyn Garden City, which were mirrored across the ICI Group in England. As a Director, I quickly became aware of the many alternatives at which I could have lunch. At the very top end was the Chairman's lunch room, followed by the "Directors' Bar" where one could order sandwiches or a snack, followed by the Senior Managers' dining room, the Visitors' luncheon room, the staff cafeteria, and finally the staff bar where pies were available.

In addition there was "Digswell Lodge" in an old thatched farmhouse near the main site (which incidentally I managed to save from destruction when a major re-development was proposed). "Digswell" was the sole preserve of the Directors and provided excellent meals accompanied by the best of wines, with some limited accommodation upstairs for visitors. The facility was used frequently by the Board, and also to entertain visitors to Plastics Division. Each of ICI's Divisions had such special facilities, and I have memories of negotiating the narrow country lanes back to St Albans after many late dinners!

The range of eating places at work underlined the class system entrenched in England.

The eating arrangements were very different in North America where alcohol was banned at lunch, and was only available at dinners which included visitors.

The English class structure was also prevalent then at ICI. This was exemplified for me when John Gadsby, the Plasics Division Personnel director, said at one of my initial lunches at Digswell Lodge,

"Ben, you realise there are four of us now?" To which, mystified, I replied

"Four?

John then said,

"You know, four of us from Oxford and Cambridge."

16

ICI Americas

After the extended 6 years with ICI's Plastics Division in England, we expected to return to Melbourne but it was not to be, as Dirk Zeidler, ICI Australia's Chairman, believed I was too young, aged 48, to join his board. In contrast the ICI Board in London were willing to offer me a senior international role.

We decided to accept an ICI offer but only with the proviso that the family would not wish to be sent to certain countries such as Japan and Nigeria, and they indicated they would keep me in Europe.

Bob Haslam, then Deputy Chairman of ICI, went out of his way to keep us fully informed of the deliberations in London as well as ICIANZ which would affect us.

London soon offered me a role not in Europe but as Senior Vice President of ICI Americas, in the United States. At the time Haslam was the ICI Board Director responsible for the Americas.

We accepted this move to Delaware, but Margaret was of course very upset when we then visited Melbourne briefly to sell our Fordholm Road home for $125,000 AUD, to a Melbourne City Councillor, Basil Elms.

Almost immediately after this I received two ICI job offers, the first from Tom Hutchison by then Chairman of Plastics Division, who asked me to become his deputy at Welwyn Garden City. I liked Tom and would have enjoyed working with him, but the US job had greater appeal and I had by then been working six years at WGC.

More surprisingly only two months later was a call I received in the middle of the night from Zeidler, who offered me a directorship on his ICIANZ board. I was annoyed and said that we had sold our Melbourne home and had accepted by then the job in the United States.

I thereby, for the first time, severed my association with Australia's senior management. We regretted Zeidler had not made the offer earlier, and I was exasperated at his approach. However I also knew that I would not have been happy working for him, but was unaware that my new American boss, Tom Maloney was a difficult and unattractive personality.

Maloney was a street fighter who had put himself through college playing basketball and sleeping in the back of his car. He appeared to have no conscience or scruples, and employed every ruse to advance his career. Maloney was extremely difficult to work for, but basked in the patronage of ICI Americas Chairman Ed Goett.

However I had some revenge later when Goett retired and recommended to the London ICI board that Maloney was the best person to succeed him. At that time there were two senior executive VP's, Tom Maloney and Harry

Corless. I told London that I would resign if Tom was made chairman and Harry was duly appointed, possibly influenced by my stance. Within a few days Maloney resigned.

With hindsight I was possibly remiss in not voicing any reservations I had about Corless. However ICI may well have appointed him being an Englishman!

I waited a further three years before becoming chairman in 1989 when Harry retired.

In 1982 the chairmanship of ICI in London changed from Maurice Hodgson (who was almost blind!) to John Harvey-Jones who with much energy breathed new life into the Company. Maurice was extremely intelligent but reticent, which could not be said of his wife!

Margaret and I attended a dinner in New York with other ICI bigwigs when Hodgson visited the United States in 1980. Mrs Hodgson arrived at the dinner with a broken arm (rumoured to have occurred when she fell down the stairs of their ICI London flat after a few drinks!) and her arm was supported with a dark silk halter scarf. During the dinner the scarf slipped off. I was sitting next to her and she asked me to look for the scarf among the many legs under the table. I came up for air and apologised that I could not see the scarf in the darkness, to which she said that I better find it! Some of my worst moments in ICI were not business related!

Harvey-Jones had a colourful career before his meteoric rise in ICI. Born in India he became a British navy lieutenant serving in submarines. Being fluent in Russian and German he worked for MI5 during the war and was attached to Tito's guerrilla headquarters in Yugoslavia, at the end of the war.

As his daughter had polio, he decided to retire from government service and joined ICI as a "time and motion" analyst. With his long hair, loud ties and jovial directness, he made an instant impression.

When he became Chairman, ICI was making a loss, "bleeding heavily from the harsh effects of Margaret Thatcher's economic policies on manufacturing", and he described the Prime Minister as Britain's greatest manufacturing handicap!

We were honoured in 1987 when unexpectedly we were invited to travel to England to sit at his table for his ICI retirement dinner held at Cliveden (made famous by the "Profumo" affair, when the names of Valerie Hobson, Christine Keeler and Dr Ward and their nude swims in the garden pool of the Manor made newspaper headlines), where we stayed the night. Harvey-Jones was unable to hide his emotions and in the middle of his retirement speech began to cry and sat down.

He was one of the great leaders I was fortunate to meet in my career. His outspokenness resulted in Margaret Thatcher refusing him a Knighthood on his retirement, but this was perhaps also influenced by the fact that ICI had refused to employ Thatcher when she graduated from university with a chemistry degree.

Harvey-Jones died in 2008, following his successful BBC series as a company "Trouble Shooter." It is interesting that he died within days of ICI's name disappearing on the stock exchange, as a result of being taken over by the Dutch company AKZO. "The Company had begun to unravel within ten years of his departure, when a threatened bid from the corporate raider Hanson exposed its weaknesses and being loaded with debt after an expensive foray into specialty chemicals"[20]

In 1992 I was asked to head Canadian Industries Limited (CIL), ICI's 73% owned company in Canada.

This meant moving to Toronto and that I would be able to see Margaret, Maggie and Lucy only on weekends.

One of ICI America's two planes (a "Falcon 50" but usually the smaller "Falcon 10") would fly me to Wilmington on Friday nights returning Sunday evening to Toronto where I rented a flat on the shore of Lake Ontario.

I was told by ICI to straighten out the Canadian company, following which I would also be appointed chairman of ICI Americas based in Wilmington. I therefore had a double incentive to get the job done.

Two senior vice presidents were terminated and several operating divisions sold. These included Chemetics, a process engineering company based in Vancouver, a plastics business in Edmonton, and a sulphuric acid business based on nickel smelter gas at several Canadian mines.

It was a very busy but satisfying year.

Canadians are very much like Australians and I enjoyed working with them. They are generally more relaxed than American businessmen who tend to be more aggressive, believing this demonstrates competence. Toronto is more English than American, and its citizens are very conscious of the frontier that lies 90 minutes down the highway, and

20 The Economist 1/1/2008. p 87

their television programmes are American. But surprisingly Toronto had entire suburbs of Chinese emigrants who moved to Canada from Hong Kong because of the impending Chinese takeover of that island.

Toronto had a distinctive Victorian flavour and I experienced this first-hand when I was made a member of the leading Toronto Club.

CIL was a major Canadian company with a history going back to the early building of the Canadian Pacific railway across the country made possible with the company's explosives. And not surprisingly, CIL's then chief executive Chuck Hantho, was Chairman of Canada's Business Council.

Margaret would occasionally accompany me and on one occasion we attended an auction and successfully bid for a French antique mirror (now in our South Yarra toilet) and came back with us to the United States on the Company "Falcon". The plane would be met at Wilmington's small airport by a customs official who came to know me and greeted me as "The Good Doctor".

While in Canada we attended the Canadian Grand Prix which was won that year by Nigel Mansell in a McLaren car, sponsored by ICI with the roundel prominently displayed on the car's bonnet. Mansell gave a presentation the day before the race for our customers. He explained the gear changes and speeds he had to make and although wearing leather gloves his hand would be bleeding after 4000 gear changes during the race.

Today's cars have eliminated this problem by having a lever on the steering wheel to change gears. Mansell also described the bruises he would suffer during a race, particularly at Brands Hatch in England where the track was very rough.

We were invited to the pit before the race because of our sponsorship. Despite the interest of meeting Mansell, we did not enjoy the deafening roar and engine wails of the race, and to this day continue to dislike the Grand Prix races at Albert Park which we can hear every year from our home in South Yarra.

In mid 1981 I was approached a second time by Milton Bridgland, then Chairman of ICI Australia, sounding me out about returning to Melbourne as a director of the company in early 1982.

Extensive correspondence continued for several months to address the many issues, which would face the family if we returned. These included salary, the cost of purchasing a home for, say, $300,000 and any support I would receive as interest rates were then over 11%, and possible Company assistance with the continuing education of Anna aged 22, then at Oxford, Mark 20 at Liverpool, and Michael 19 at the University of Colorado.

The educational costs of these three totalled some $12,000 AUD per year and this was readily absorbed within my US salary. Bridgland suggested the educational expenses "would not be a problem" but the salary he offered me was $90,000 to $100,000.

It became clear that our income would go down significantly, and after much family discussion I declined a return to the Board in Australia.

No further return offers came our way, which was not

surprising. Furthermore ICI Americas were keen for me to stay and I retired there in 1993.

A flavour of our life in the United States is captured in Margaret's letter to the children in March 1986:

Dear Children,

We are so scattered around the world, Daddy and I thought about writing a family journal, so I am starting in Feb. 1986, on the train from Washington to Wilmington. The year started well.

Daddy and I plus Maggie and Lucy drove to New York, staying of course at the Olympic Towers, courtesy of the Imperial Chemist. We were joined by Benny and Jeanine. We dropped in for tea in Greenwich Village to meet George's mother, (George being Maggie's boyfriend).

New Year's eve we saw Noel Coward's 'Hay Fever', after which we wandered to Times Square to see the New Year in, but the crowd was pretty scary, noisy, many, many police with truncheons, not to mention drunks etc. We returned to the apartment to watch the Big Apple drop on TV. The following night, we had dinner with Jan, Cary, Ben, Jeanine and Lucy, at an Italian restaurant, good food, and talked about old times, and absent children such as Mike and Benny on their walkabouts in Melbourne, the raiding of letter boxes around Hawthorn to collect stamps, the Home in Fordholm road. It was a good though tiring weekend. We walked to the National Art Gallery on the way spent an hour in a shop that specialised in music boxes etc. and I had to do the sales in Saks. (I didn't get my nickname Black Belt Shopper for nothing!).

The next memory was a four-day visit to Boca Raton, Florida at the end of January. We left Delaware on the Company plane in freezing conditions, snow storms, me in my new mink jacket, but nevertheless very worried about ice forming on the plane's wings.
I guess I read too many novels.
We also saw the new plane in the hangar ICI recently bought, larger, more comfortable, with kitchen facilities, and should be in operation later this month.

Lucy once again left in the tender care of Mrs Kallfelz, not too happily. The weather in Florida was perfect, spent the first day around the pool, lavish dinners every night, tennis for me during the day, but work for Daddy, a typical American convention scene. I flew home on the Sunday, but Daddy went direct from Miami to London, once again on Concord. I now have a collection of grey tennis socks, grey being the Concord flight slipper colour.

No snow over Christmas but we made up for it in Jan and Feb, normally I would have been confined to the house, but because of my new Plymouth Voyager, front wheel drive, I drove Lucy to school on days when the school buses didn't run and all schools closed, i.e. except Tower Hill which never closes.

Feb 11th, a party at Kuons to meet a visiting Chinese composer Du Ming-Xin and his wife, who were the guest of honour the following Sunday in Washington, organised by the Deleware Symphony orchestra, called

"A Caravan to Kennedy". We left on a special train at 9.30, a band playing on the platform "Chatanooga Choo Choo" and other music. 400 of us with eskis, champagne, etc, for the trip home. We were part of a large group of Delewareans, 2100 in all who converged on Washington by train, bus and private transport.

Our first stop was lunch at the Chinese embassy, then a reception at the Kennedy Centre, then the concert. The main event a violin concerto composed by Du Ming-Xin. We had Sen. Joe Biden's seats and sat next to Eisenhower's granddaughter. We then boarded our special train for a most enjoyable trip home.

Daddy left for London the next day, and managed to fit in a visit to Amsterdam, had dinner with Big Ben to sort out trip to Indonesia – a sentimental journey for both Bens. To revisit parts of Sumatra and Java, and hopefully to locate grandfather Lochtenberg's grave.

Our next trip was to Toronto, my first time in Canada. We stayed at the Four Seasons, a lovely hotel, and truly one of the best shopping areas I've ever seen.

Now re: our trip, we leave on March 31st by JAL stopping in Tokyo, and meet Big Ben and Charlotte in Singapore on April 4th at Raffles. Lucy's birthday on the 3rd, we plan to celebrate before we leave Wilmington. Lucy will stay at the Kuons while we are away.

We will be visiting Medan, Brastigi, Samosin island, Parapet, back to Medan, fly to Jakarta, then by car to Samudra, Bandung then on to Bali.

We arrive in Sydney on 16th of April at 8-10am. Hope

Anna or Mark will be able to meet us. We then go onto Melbourne, and leave Australia Sun 20th for Denpasser, not long in Australia. Just time for us to see Anna and Nick, Mark and Ab, Mike and Jen, and Gran. We then have three days in Bali, a well-deserved holiday for Daddy, then straight home nonstop, arriving 25th of April. Enough time I hope for me to hire a truck, polish furniture, clean brass and silver, pack up and drive to Bethesda, my first real, and I think prestigious, antiques fair. Had a letter from John Lynch to announce his travel plans and expect him to arrive Wilmington 26th April, the worst time for us to have guests, but we'll survive.

My recent part time job as a volunteer for St Francis hospital: I install "Life Line" units in people's homes, where they have emergency buttons. It requires two visits, the first to check condition of patient, medications etc, and type of phone jack. This is followed by installation itself, instruction, making sure they have three sponsors etc. It takes more time than I thought, but I enjoy it more than meals on wheels, where I was getting lost.

Jan was voted top of his class of associates, and was well rewarded. Cary is anxiously awaiting the birth of Thomasina's 2nd baby.

Anna and Nick are also "expecting". They are all well and happy. I am to be a grandmother at last, baby due about Oct. They now own their house, Nick very busy working and redecorating.

Mark and Abigail are both working, Mark with Peko Wallsend. According to Anna, the way he talks about work, is becoming more like Dad every day. Ab is working in a law firm.

Now for Mick. We hear nothing but good reports via Chris Grieve. According to Gran, Mick was in a car accident but was not hurt. Also Jen is not happy in Australia and is returning to America.

Ben is playing rugby all over the country and will be home this weekend. He is busy with job interviews and so is in need of prayers please.

Maggie is having her ups and downs. She was home 2 weeks ago as she was not well, shaking off the flu.
There is some talk of her going on holiday with George during Spring break. Maggie is hoping to do a French course in Paris this summer.

Lucy is busy with school, piano and sports. This season she plays lacrosse and today after school, we are going to buy a lacrosse stick. Last week she went with the school to Washington. She said it was AWFUL AWFUL AWFUL. Never the less she appears to have seen and taken in a lot. According to Lucy they spent two nights in a crummy hotel.

I went to Washington yesterday on a bus with a group of women, to see an exhibit called "The Treasure Houses of Britain". I enjoyed the exhibit, but didn't know any of the women, was the only smoker and sat on my own at the back of the bus, felt an outcast.

We 3 at home send our love. Daddy and I are looking forward to our trip to Indonesia and Australia. I hope to repeat this journal every few months, but please God my typing improves. This letter has taken hours.

Our love to you all, Mummy, Daddy and Lucy.

An unexpected and bizarre sequel to my 1972 visit to China occurred in the 1980s when I was Chairman of ICI Americas in Wilmington. Until then I had been working in the United States as an Australian citizen with a "Green Card" which designated me a resident alien.

I also had a "black" or top security clearance from the Government because ICI Americas had a subsidiary "Fiberite Inc" which it had acquired from Beatrice Chemicals Inc. "Fiberite" made carbon fibre for the US Air Force stealth bomber and stealth fighter, as well as the exhaust nozzles for NASA's space shuttle rocket.

What has all this to do with China?

Well, at that time the United States top secret technology for silent submarine propellers was lost to the Russians as a result of a leak by Toshiba through a Norwegian intermediary. Within days, all resident aliens lost their security clearance and so did I.

ICI Americas were in danger of losing their Air Force stealth fighter and bomber contract and it was proposed that this could be avoided if I became a United States citizen. As a precursor for this a CIA agent came from Washington to interview me in Wilmington to assess whether I could proceed with my citizenship application and have my security clearance restored.

The interview started with the agent making me swear that I would never divulge the interview proceedings. With hindsight I now understand why he demanded this.

He started by asking me how many relations I had living in China. I replied, "None." To which he attempted to clarify, "Are you telling me, they are all dead?"

I said I never to my knowledge ever had any relatives in China and this resulted in an incredulous reaction by the agent, "But you were born in China" he exclaimed. I replied, "No, I was born in Singapore" to which the agent said, "But Singapore is in China."

Fortunately despite this exchange, I soon received USA citizenship and my security clearance was restored.

Margaret and I enjoyed our home at Chadds Ford on Kennett Pike, and tennis friends we met at the Greenville Country Club, which was located about a mile from our home. One day while driving and enjoying my white Chrysler convertible into the club with the hood down, two lady members called out to me, "Last flicker of male menopause!"

Our home was set on three acres of grass, which in summer had to be mowed weekly by tractor, a task Michael and Benedict enjoyed. It was a peaceful oasis for the family with its pool that froze in winter and with wild life ranging from deer and fireflies glowing at dusk. Unhappily my car injured a deer as I was entering our drive and I had to call a ranger to kill the animal.

A lasting memory was of the thousands of Canada geese flying over our home in V formation and honking, as they headed south in autumn.

A couple we knew in Wilmington were Sam and Roxanne Arsht. Both were judges at the Delaware Chancery court which specialised in commercial litigation throughout the

United States, as most of the Fortune 500 Companies were registered in Delaware. The Arsht's had privately funded and established a Centre of Life-long Learning, and Margaret attended some art classes there. Their only child and daughter, Adrienne, lived in Washington and also became a friend.

On her periodic visits to her parents in Wilmington, Adrienne would bring us gifts of bread and nightdresses from a bakery and dress shop she owned in Washington. We stayed with her and her husband, Myer Feldman, in their home on a visit we made to the Capital.

Feldman was a very interesting person having been Ted Sorenson's assistant in the Kennedy White House, despite having been raised in a Philadelphia orphanage.

At Kennedy's time White House staff totalled some 25, and lived in the President's home. Today the White House staff total several hundred and are accommodated in a nearby building.

Myer told us he had kept a document which declared war by the United States on Russia, signed by Kennedy during the Cuban Missile Crisis. The document had some water stains as Myer had taken it to the President to sign while he was having a bath. Kennedy joked that people might one day think that he was crying when he signed the document!

Feldman headed a law firm of some one hundred lawyers, and also shared a diamond import business with his friend Maurice Templeman, who squired Jackie Kennedy after she divorced Onassis. Feldman offered to introduce us to Jackie, but unfortunately this never eventuated.

Near our Chadds Ford home was the house formerly owned by Jim Thompson, who died mysteriously in 1967 in a Malayan jungle, reportedly employed by the CIA. He had started a Thai silk business in his Bangkok home that bears his name to this day, which we have visited. Also near us in Chadds Ford lived Andrew Wyeth. When attending a party there, he agreed to sign a print we had of "Christina's World", but unfortunately was stopped by his wife.

One of the challenges of my Senior VP years from 1979 to 1988 was my involvement in the Corpus Christi cracker in Texas, jointly owned by the Belgian company Solway, the US company Union Pacific Railway and ICI.

The experience put me off joint ventures forever as it was difficult and sometimes impossible to get agreement on a major issue. Board meetings often ended in open hostility.

The ICI London chairman, John Harvey-Jones, visited the Texas plant but did not help motivate the staff when he said to managers,

"Who the hell decided to build this cathedral in the desert!".

I also became heavily involved in the ICI purchase of Beatrice Chemicals for $750 million, comprising a group of nine separate companies which were much more customer focussed and decentralised than ICI. Each Beatrice Company was run by an independent general manager who was measured only by his bottom line results. The purchase was made when John Harvey-Jones was chairman, and Brian Smith had replaced Bob Haslam as ICI director responsible for the Americas and was based in New York.

The jewel among the companies bought from Beatrice was Stahl Chemicals, which was the world leader in leather finishes and regularly made a profit not less than 23%.

Stahl's general manager was Joe Ossoff, a motivational Jewish leader who ran the business as if it was his own. Other companies included Fiberite, which manufactured carbon fibre, used in stealth fighters and bombers, Converters Printing Inks, Imperial Oil and Grease, and Thoro waterproof sealants.

The Beatrice companies had operations throughout the United States as well as some in Europe. I replaced the Beatrice chief executive who was retired, and very much enjoyed working with these managers. I moved to Boston for twelve months after the purchase and rented an apartment near the harbour, returning to Chadds Ford most weekends.

However the entrepreneurial flair of the group did not survive after Dennis Henderson replaced John Harvey-Jones as ICI chairman. Dennis insisted that the Beatrice procedures and information systems which were tailored to their individual businesses be changed to the centralised ICI accounting system, despite my protests.

We travelled a great deal on business throughout the United States and even occasionally to Mexico, Brazil and Argentina. Margaret accompanied me on the longer overseas trips, and often when we hosted visiting senior ICI couples such as the Hendersons and Hampels, or to attend industry functions.

One of the Chemicals Manufacturers Association meetings involved staying at the St. Regis in New York and a day trip on the "Highlander" owned by Steve Forbes. We cruised up the Hudson to see an Army-Navy football game at the army academy at West Point.

There was entertainment on the trip back to Manhattan

and as innocents we got caught in a solo card game with cardsharps who included Caspar Weinberger, then Secretary of Defence, who cleaned us out of our cash!

We made a memorable trip to Buenos Aries in Argentina to visit Tommy Hudson, the "Duperial" Managing Director.

The Company's name derived from the earlier formation of a joint venture between Dupont and ICI. Tommy although a third or fourth generation Argentinian, was more English than the British! He was an experienced Polo player as well as a member of Leander rowing club in Henley.

Our visit included a journey to Salsa in the Andes and Iguazu Falls, which adjoins Uruguay, Brazil and Argentina.

In Buenos Aries we stayed at the hotel, which was then hosting a visit of Francois Mitterrand then President of France. There were many red faces including Mitterand's as the flags in front of the hotel to celebrate his arrival, were mistakenly Italian instead of French! Needless to say, the hotel was swarming with security personnel.

In Rio, we stayed at the Copacabana Palace hotel near the glamorous beach, but also facing inland hills crowded with the favela slums of the poor. We made an interesting trip to the north and the old city of Salvadore where we stayed in a hotel that was previously a convent.

Our lives were very comfortable with the use of the Company's two planes, which would fly me from Wilmington to the BA terminal at JFK for Concorde departures and arrivals. I made thirty-one such trips across the Atlantic to London in the year 1990!

On my return I would be cleared by a single customs official at Wilmington airport, who would come into the

ICI plane with the greeting, "Hello again Dr Lochtenberg, anything to declare this trip?"

I was able to lend our "Falcon" aircraft on one occasion to Paul Volcker, then Chairman of the US Federal Reserve, who having missed his connection in New York was then able to attend a dinner in Wilmington hosted by Dupont.

In his speech that night, Volcker gave special praise to a great chemical company, at which the Duponters began to smile.

But Volcker ended his sentence to the dismay of his hosts with "ICI" and not "Dupont"! (Volcker has been prominent in the Australian press by revealing the $US 220 million kickbacks to Sadam Hussein by the Australian Wheat Board, during the Iraq "Food for Oil Programme").

Margaret and I also made good use of the ICI flats in the Olympic Tower on 51st Street New York, and also in Arlington Street London near the Ritz Hotel corner of Piccadilly.

Near the latter ICI flat was 'The Caprice' restaurant reportedly frequented by Princess Diana.

We were regularly invited to Wimbledon as ICI had responsibility for maintaining the grass courts throughout the tournament. Such events were not always enjoyable as one year it rained continually, and we entertained our customers by watching films of previous tournaments during our lunch in the ICI tent.

Such aspects of our life in the United States were luxurious in every sense, but we have not missed these perks since our return to Australia in 1993. We did enjoy meeting famous leaders at functions such as at the British embassy in Washington (formerly the home of World War's General

Patton) where we met Queen Elizabeth (who is remarkably short), Margaret Thatcher and later Benazir Bhutto in Philadelphia.

In 1988 we joined Frank Costigan and Ruth Jones for a holiday in Italy and Israel. We met in Naples, staying at the Excelsior Hotel, which was part of the Sheraton Group. Ruth at the time was a manager at the Sheraton Hotel in Melbourne, and she had arranged for us to have VIP attention.

We arrived before Ruth and Frank, and were shown into a magnificent suite with windows facing Vesuvius, across Naples bay. When Ruth and Frank arrived later we joined them in their room, and it became a source of ribbing as their room was inferior to ours!

This occurred again when we travelled by car to Ravello and stayed at a delightful hotel, when they were shown a room smaller than ours. The four of us went to the front desk, and dignity was restored when they were moved to a better room.

We travelled next to Jerusalem and stayed in the Arab area outside the city walls at the hotel called 'The American Colony', as an American Missionary had founded it. The trip was a great success, and together we visited several biblical sites as well as Amman and Petra.

The family also holidayed on a skippered boat from Tortola in the Virgin Islands, joined by Benedict, Jeanine, Maggie and Lucy, and on our own on the 'Little Dix Rock Resort' in the Carribean.

Of our various functions and visits to New York, one in June 1993, relates to our later life in Australia. Being an Australian executive working in the United States, we were invited to a drinks party of the 'Australian American Leadership Dialogue' founded by Phil Scanlon.

The party was held in Richard Pratt's 5th Avenue apartment, evidence if needed of the latter's political network. The Dialogue is a yearly meeting of politicians and business leaders aimed at strengthening informal links between the two countries. Among the Australians at this meeting were Nick Bolkus and Kim Beazley.

I learned recently that Kevin Rudd and Therese Rein were also present, the latter pregnant with her first child.[21]

Unfortunately we did not meet our future Prime Minister, or his wife, that night.

Another interesting and satisfying task was membership of the Rhodes Selection Committee for New York, Pennsylvania, Delaware, Maryland, Virginia and West Virginia. Our annual meeting interviewed candidates from the six States to select four Rhodes Scholars. Each State had one representative Rhodes Scholar, and I was fortunate being the only Scholar resident working in Delaware.

The real joy of being on the committee was its chair Tim Healey, the Jesuit Rector of Georgetown University in Washington.

Healey was a gentle but formidable inquisitor who quickly exposed any weakness in the candidate's written application or interview. We met in his book-lined apartment off 5th Avenue, as he had also been appointed Chairman of the New York Library.

I learned much from Healey during my three years membership of the committee.

---

21 'Kevin Rudd' by Robert Macklin 2007. p 122 - 124

While still in the USA, ICI suffered a major scare in 1991 when Britain's leading corporate raiders Lord Hanson, and Gordon White, of Hanson Trust bought 2.8% of ICI's shares. Panic erupted in Millbank and a campaign involving Goldman Sachs was launched to discredit Hanson. The defence was successful as it exposed Hanson's accounts to be a pack of cards, and that White had bought his yacht and race horses with company funds.

The episode awakened ICI from its slumbers and led to the separation of the pharmaceuticals division and subsequent transformation of ICI from a basic to a specialty chemicals company.

A comment about working for an British or foreign Company in the United States:

As CEO of a major chemicals company I was a member of the Board of the Chemicals Manufacturers Association. However, I was excluded from critical strategic CMA discussions, as were representatives of other foreign companies such as Bayer, BASF and Hoechst.

My last major task as ICI Americas chairman was to oversee this hiving-off and separation of the pharmaceuticals business which was then predominantly centred in the USA.

The United States operation involved a large research centre in Wilmington and a sales force of 1000 medical sales staff. The project required significant interaction with government regulators such as Department of Justice in Washington and the EPA, which approved new drugs and operating licences.

The newly separated company from ICI was named "Zeneca", which was to merge later with the Swedish company "Astra".

At the time of the split ICI shares in London were £8, whereas they languished below £4 when they were later taken over by 'Akzo Nobel'. 'Astra-Zeneca' shares later were over £30!

My ICI Americas retirement came with a rush and involved the packing of our furniture and belongings as well as sale of our Chadds Ford home.

We moved temporarily into the Hotel Dupont, and while there Lucy arrived unexpectedly from Australia and had to sleep on the couch in our suite. She had gone to Sydney in preference to our earlier offer that she join the Peace Corps.

She had stayed in Sydney with Mark, but decided to return and resume her studies at the University of Pennsylvania.

The ICI Americas staff organised a farewell party for us in the company cafeteria, and the very next day we departed Philadelphia airport for Australia.

It was an immediate clean break, as I did not wish to repeat what my predecessor, Harry Corless had done.

After my appointment as chairman, Corless would return repeatedly with personal requests that irritated me especially my secretary Mercina Gant.

A negative in my final jobs as ICI Canada president and ICI Americas chairman was that I reported to Ronnie Hampel, a London based director who later became chairman of ICI. Hampel had boundless energy and commercial acumen and was extremely ambitious and political. He grudgingly respected those who stood up to him and this small group included Margaret.

I was more fortunate in my career to have worked for ICI leaders such as Archie Glenn, John Harvey-Jones, Bob

Haslam and Brian Smith, and ended my executive career in fulfilling and satisfying years as ICI Americas Chairman.

Hampel's business ethos was exemplified in the way he treated ICI America's retirees. He ensured the pension of USA based employees was frozen at retirement (including unfortunately mine), whereas UK based retirees continue to be indexed with inflation.

I believe this discriminatory treatment of US based employees would not have occurred when Harvey-Jones or Haslam were on the ICI Board.

Hampel also attempted to have my ICI share options cancelled when I retired. Fortunately I became aware of this, and I alerted the two ICI Americas non-executive directors Paul Montrone and Tom Wyman. The two and Hampel comprised the ICI Americas compensation committee. Fortunately they over-ruled Hampel, so I retired with my share options intact.

17

Retirement to
Australia in 1993

A year before my retirement in 1993, I was asked by ICI London to join the ICI Australia board in Melbourne. I jumped at this opportunity as it provided me with a re-entry into business in Australia.

Although it involved a year of tiring monthly flights from Philadelphia for board meetings in Melbourne, I accepted this travel burden happily. Once settled back in Melbourne this led later to becoming Chairman of ICI Australia in1995 and I held this position until I retired from the company in 2001.

ICI London as major shareholder attempted to control ICI Australia through representatives on the Melbourne board, often to the disadvantage of the Australian shareholders. This came to a head when I was Chairman when they asked me to terminate the chief executive Warren Haynes.

I saw no reasonable basis for taking this action, and told London that I would resign if they wished to pursue this.

The ICI Australia board had some lively members including Bill Dix, ex- CEO of Ford Australia, Geoff Healey previously finance director of BHP, and Cathy Walter who later precipitated the resignation of the whole NAB board of which she was a member. I was closest to Tony Daniels, also a director of CBA and AGL, and whom I had got to know on the "Capral" Board. I had hoped Tony would be my successor as Chairman when I retired, but he was disinclined and the board then appointed Don Mercer, who had joined the board after falling out with the ANZ chairman Charles Goode, when he was the bank's CEO.

The interests I developed following our return to Melbourne in 1993 were very satisfying and enjoyable. Activities such as the Mental Health Research Institute and the Council of the University of Melbourne were challenging but not stressful.

In these new roles I met a cross section of interesting and stimulating other professionals. And importantly, my arthritis, which resulted in me leaving Wilmington on walking sticks, left me within a couple of years of my retirement.

No longer under stress at work, I also benefitted considerably from the treatment prescribed by my specialist Stephen Hall and Margaret's care and attention with my diet.

In contrast, the Canadian and United States doctors in earlier years had been unable to relieve my arthritis except for diagnosing it to be psoriatic.

I am now free of arthritis, but remember having to visit Stephen Hall to receive cortisone injections in my right hand so that I could shake hands with those receiving degrees at University of Melbourne graduation ceremonies.

Back in Australia I accepted directorships in the Alcan Company 'Capral' in Sydney and later the internet travel company 'Webjet' in Melbourne. June Zeidler, wife of Dirk, was then secretary of the Mental Health Research Institute asked me to join that board. I agreed and at my first MHRI board meeting, after several minutes asked, "When do we start?" Only to be told that this was up to me as I was chairman! I had not realised that Richard Pratt who was the founding Chairman of MHRI had resigned, and was caught completely by surprise. I continued for ten years as MHRI Chairman experiencing many positives as well as some negatives.

On the plus side was working with Dame Margaret Guilfoyle, an ex-Federal Minister of Health, and avuncular Tom Molomby from the law firm started by he and his brother.

But there was growing frustration with the Institute Director Dr David Copolov who was good hearted, totally committed and a great ambassador and fundraiser for the Institute.

I sought advice from Gus Nossal director of the Walter and Eliza institute, and asked Jack Martin from St. Vincent's Research Institute to review MHRI's operations and direction. My MHRI involvement resulted in me being appointed in 1995 by then Victorian Minister of Health, Marie Tehan, to chair a committee reviewing remuneration of medical staff in Victorian public hospitals.

Committee members included David Pennington then Vice Chancellor of the University of Melbourne, John McNeil a professor of public health at Monash, and Bob Dickens, the senior paediatric surgeon at the Royal Children's Hospital.

The committee recommended a significant increase in salaries, which was approved by Kennett's Government.

The work exposed me to city and country hospitals and I found these visits extremely interesting. Pennington subsequently recommended that I be appointed a member of the University of Melbourne Council.

The medical remuneration committee's work was followed by a Government restructuring of the whole Victorian public hospital system and existing hospital boards were swept away and replaced by several new 'network' boards, each comprising up to five or six hospitals.

I was invited to join the 'Eastern Network', which included St Vincent's, the Alfred, Box Hill amongst other hospitals. I was surprised to find that this Board did not include any members with medical backgrounds, but was primarily drawn from business and commerce.

It was a learning experience for me, and frequently I had to ask my wife Margaret to explain medical terms to me.

Membership of the University of Melbourne Council introduced me to a wide range of outstanding Council members, academics and university administrators, including later High Court Judge Susan Crennan, Vice Chancellor Glyn Davis, Chancellors Faye Marles and Ian Renard, Deputy Chancellor Alex Chernov (later Governor of Victoria), and Rosa Storelli, headmistress of Methodist Ladies College.

They were an extremely committed and hard working group. I enjoyed eleven years on the Council, the last two years as Deputy Chancellor. The University graciously awarded me a Honorary Degree of Doctor of Laws on my retirement from the University in March 2007.

So despite being overseas for twenty years, one activity fortuitously led to another following our return to Australia.

I count myself fortunate as these retirement activities were very satisfying, and kept me out of Margaret's hair!

She in turn enjoyed her return to Melbourne where many of her nursing friends had settled, some having married doctors from St. Vincent. It also made me wonder whether I should have retired earlier from ICI Americas, although I have no regrets.

We had bought "Emerton" in Domain Road in South Yarra for $1,450,000 following countless property inspection visits to Melbourne from the United States by Margaret during 1992. We purchased our new home a year before our return by agreeing a peppercorn rental with the vendor Don Musto.

We re-established contact with our 'Teams of Our Lady' friends who included the Costigans (who unhappilly had divorced while we were overseas), and Francis Weston, Max having died.

All in all we were very happy to be back in Australia and soon added an extension to our new home for $145,000.

This included a studio/study for Margaret, a small exercise pool for my arthritis and to loosen our joints, as well as a garage/storeroom. We were fortunate in being able to employ as the architect, Nonda Katsilides who had added the second floor to the original ballroom of the house in 1982. Katsalides had by then restricted his work to high-rise city buildings. However he agreed to do our extension because of his earlier involvement with the property. 'Emerton' had an interesting history, the site being originally a tennis court for the Melbourne colonial lawyer Emerton who lived in the adjoining house.

Emerton's daughter who became Dame Mabel Brooks, wrote in her autobiography:

"Daddy built himself a billiard room and me a ballroom"

In addition to our pool and studio extension, we later in 2007 added a lift to service the garage/pool, the ballroom, the studio and finally my study and the bedroom floor.

The lift helped us with the stairs, and this became doubly important after Margaret had a fall down the main flight of stairs. It was a major project taking 12 months, as we upgraded the kitchen and also changed a small upstairs bathroom into a reading room to link our bedroom and my study. We had a wonderful builder, Jamie Smarrelli who coped with endless difficulties, particularly when cutting into walls and the roof for the lift.

At the same time, in our "Carmel" unit in Broadbeach Queensland, we merged one bedroom into an enlarged living area, and upgraded the kitchen. Unfortunately, our Queensland builder was a villain which was stressful and Margaret had to make several trips to Qld. The end result of our changes, particularly in Domain Road, is very good and we love living opposite the Botanical Gardens and a nearby shopping village. Our wonderful neighbours Maria and Martin Ryan are an added bonus. At the time of this writing this, Domain Road at 22 years has been longest stay in our many homes!

In our travels we have collected an eclectic range of objects and paintings, although none of great value. We have a range of antique furniture, silver and glass as a result of Margaret's business ownership of 'Ashwell Antiques' and her earlier studies at the V & A in London.

Some of our possessions illustrate the many skills and crafts which have been lost, whether gold foil on the mercury backed French mirror in our front hall, or the Parian statues which grace the top of our library bookcase.

Parian was developed in England from the established European chalky biscuit or bisque porcelain, and both Minton and Copeland claim to have invented this denser and more marble-like quality in the late 1840s.

Parian has a lustrous quality and is creamy or pure white. Heavy shrinkage occurs at the first and later firings, reducing the model by up to a quarter or even a third. Models were often drawn from classical art as well as public figures. Production of Parian was discontinued in the early 1900s because of the cost.

On our return to Australia Margaret and I became involved in charitable causes such as refugees and the homeless. The homeless project in South Yarra was started by the Parish priest Father John Barry (Margaret's cousin), and absorbed a lot of our time.

Left to Right:
Ben Lochtenberg, Father John Barry
and Margaret

The initial Chairman of "St Joseph's South Yarra Emergency Housing" was Doctor David Quinn who invited Margaret to join, and whom she succeeded after two years as Chair.

Margaret helped raise $1 million to build and fit out the first four self-contained units for the homeless, and later an additional six units in the Parish building, which was no longer operating as a school.

The unique advantage of this project is that it is hands-on, with there being no overheads as all administration, maintenance and cleaning of public areas and following a change of occupancy being done by volunteers.

The financial help we gave to these activities and also other charities led us to establish our modest "Lochtenberg Foundation", taking advantage of new Government legislation. It was possible to establish a personal Foundation by making annual cash contributions. As these contributions are tax deductible their value is doubled when one's personal tax rate is 50%. Income on investments made by the Foundation is tax-free but must be distributed each year to recognised charities.

Capital growth of the Foundation is also tax-free. We saw another advantage in setting up our foundation in that some of the family might in future also contribute or suggest charities that deserve support. Happily this further aim is being achieved.

18

Reflections

In my last years at school I began to think about what career I might follow. My Jesuit teachers suggested that I might be suited to Government diplomatic service and this possibility intrigued me, but was not pursued. Later my Oxford professor Sandy Thom wanted me to continue at Oxford and offered me a position at the Engineering School, but an academic career did not interest me despite being invited to present a paper on my thesis to the Russian Institute of Aeronautical Science in Moscow.

Thom would not permit me to accept this invitation, perhaps for British security reasons.

On my return from Oxford to Melbourne I flirted with politics and joined the small named 'Grange Road Group' in Melbourne, an informal political ginger group which included John Gorton, later to become Prime Minister, and also Andrew Peacock then the ambitious national President of the Young Liberals who later become Foreign Affairs Minister in John Howard's Government.

I attended a number of monthly meetings at private homes

to discuss current political issues. However I soon became disillusioned about following a life in politics, observing that Peacock would usually arrive late or leave early for our meetings to attend innumerable other functions and meetings to advance his political network and career.

It is not surprising that my mathematical/engineering background was uncomfortable with politics, which has been described as a compromise-ridden art of the possible.

I have asked myself why young engineer Lochtenberg continued with the ICI Group throughout his working career of 37 years ? What may have contributed to this apparent lack of initiative and inertia was the stimulus I continued to receive in a succession of ICI jobs.

My ICI jobs changed every three or four years as a result of moves or promotions. Sometimes there were major changes as when the family was moved internationally to England and later to the United States, and alone by myself to Canada. Inevitably my ICI career did include flat periods and at such times I was tempted to leave ICI.

From memory this occurred on four occasions. The first time I considered leaving was for a position advertised by the 'Australian Controls' Company chaired by the brother of then Prime Minister Robert Menzies.

However I was rejected at my very first interview, being told by Menzies that his Company was not looking for someone with my academic credentials but an entrepreneur who had 'successfully put together four or five milk bars and then floated a new Company'. Somewhat chastened by this business realism, I soldiered on with ICIANZ until a few years later when I applied for a job as an Australian Trade

Commissioner, in response to a newspaper advertisement.

The attraction was that the posting was to Stockholm and the job also involved diplomatic responsibility for East Germany, as Australia had no embassy there. The position attracted several hundred applicants, and this time I passed all the interviews and was provisionally selected subject to a final interview when they also wished to screen Margaret to be sure that she passed muster!

Little did the Deputy Head of the Trade Commissioner Service who interviewed us in Canberra realise that it was Margaret who was in fact interviewing him!

He got off to a bad start by offering me a cigarette but not to Margaret who smoked at that time, and he compounded this error when he revealed that his family owned several sets of cutlery and dinnerware bought duty-free during his many international moves, but admitted that the education of his children had suffered. Needless to say we declined the Stockholm posting.

Another time I considered leaving ICI was when I received an unsolicited offer from a head-hunter on behalf of the USA construction company Fluor, for a Vice President position at their head office in San Francisco.

This opportunity really tempted us but was overtaken by the only serious offer I considered, which I received from Western Mining's Managing Director, Arvi Parbo, to become WMC's Commercial Manager. I had got to know Parbo through selling explosives to WMC mines.

We decided to accept the WMC offer and I came to see Archie Glenn (later Sir Archiebald), then MD of ICIANZ, to tell him of my decision. Archie took the wind out of my sails as without any pause or hesitation he said as, "You are not going to join WMC but instead go to England as a director of ICI's Plastics Division".

I did not know Parbo well, but looked up to Glenn as a father figure. As a result, the meeting with Glenn led me to reverse my decision to join WMC.

What I did not appreciate at the time was that Glenn's offer to me was made without the knowledge or agreement of ICI in London to take me on as a Plastics Division director. However Glenn was then also an ICI main board director in London, and must have felt confident that he would be able to lean on the Plastics Division then Chairman Charles Vowles, to accept me.

I have often speculated on what might have eventuated for the Lochtenberg family if I had accepted Parbo's offer and not gone overseas with ICI but remained in Australia.

So Parbo, and then Glenn, really changed our lives and those of our children. We did not appreciate at the time how significant this was to be.

My career exposed me to the political and financial drivers that affect personal relationships. This was exemplified by my St. Louis school colleague Dr Harry Crock, who was unable to get a post-graduate degree from Oxford University as Oxford's then Medical Faculty Dean insisted that his name be included as a collaborator in Harry's Doctoral thesis which was to be published, as Harry's research broke new ground on the blood system in bones. Harry did not agree, and as a result left Oxford without a degree. I myself experienced this in a minor way when I did not receive a free passage from Perth to England to take up my scholarship, because of the animosity between the Vice Chancellor and my sponsor Senior Lecturer and Rhodes Scholar Gordon Barrett Hill.

Academic rivalries can be intense, as reputations, appointments and promotions often result from research sourced by funding. The pinnacle of academic success is of course a Nobel Prize. I saw such rivalry and ambition repeatedly during my time on the University of Melbourne Council and as a member of its professorial appointment committee. This funding driver also underpins the activities of the advisory board of CAPPE (Centre of Applied Philosophy and Public Ethics), of which I was a member on behalf of the University of Melbourne.

After staying with the ICI group throughout my career, I have reflected that perhaps I should have retired from ICI Americas earlier than 1993.

My "semi-retirement" since returning to Australia from full time employment has been a very happy time for both Margaret and I, stimulated by a range of new interests. Free from the daily pressure of being an executive, I have had time to reflect on what life is all about.

Although my many career moves within ICI and internationally were stimulating, broadening and rewarding, they had a significant impact on both Margaret and I. For Margaret it has meant separation from her family and a life in Melbourne with close friends. She also was subjected to the pressures of being a "corporate wife".

This necessitated having to develop new relationships successively in Scotland, England and the United States.

These can never be as deep and fulfilling as relationships, which develop when one shares with friends the challenges of nurturing and educating a growing family. There were also many occasions when I was away and Margaret had to solve family and domestic problems alone. It is perhaps difficult to now fully appreciate that this was a time when the Internet and ease of worldwide communications were still in their infancy.

Margaret also faced the repeated challenge of meeting and entertaining company customers, suppliers and colleagues she would not know, including some from Japan and Europe. These ranged from a few who became friends, but also some she had to endure.

Margaret developed other interests including a decorative arts study course at the Victoria and Albert Museum in Knightsbridge, and working in an antiques shop in St. Albans. This was owned by Josephine Graham-Ballin, who at that time ran the annual Chelsea Antiques Fair. Later in the United States she developed this interest further, opening the 'Ashwell Antiques' business at a shop on Kennett Pike in Centreville near our home in Chadds Ford.

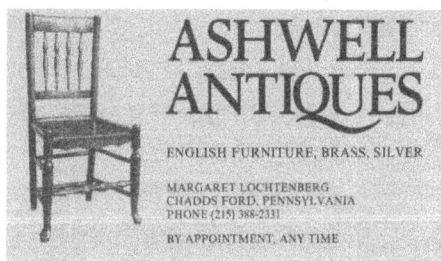

ASHWELL ANTIQUES

ENGLISH FURNITURE, BRASS, SILVER

MARGARET LOCHTENBERG
CHADDS FORD, PENNSYLVANIA
PHONE (215) 388-2331

BY APPOINTMENT, ANY TIME

The business card for Margaret's business,
"Ashwell Antiques"

This interest was supplemented by captaining a Greenville Country Club tennis team. She had also before our move to the United States single-handedly bought and restored a three story Georgian town house on Theberton Street in Islington London, which had been occupied by squatters. The latter had burnt the staircase railings and wooden window shutters for fuel in winter!

When I first visited the house, which Margaret selected, I queried the large hole in the roof, which was covered with a tarpaulin. Margaret replied that would easily be fixed by an Irish builder named Lynch, whom she had hired!

She also, to my considerable concern, removed a basement load-bearing dividing wall that was replaced with a steel beam. Margaret created a delightful pied-a-terre with its bees-wax finished wood shutters and railings, and an enlarged basement kitchen-dining area.

When we moved to the United States the house became a London base for Mark, Michael and Benedict who were at "Stonyhurst" boarding school, and also for Jan, Anna and Mark later when they attended universities in England.

As for myself, I have never felt that I belonged anywhere and have not had many opportunities therefore to develop close friendships. This is not just the result of several international moves with ICI, but also because I changed schools repeatedly in my childhood.

My initial schooling was in Batavia, now Djakarta, followed when aged 8 at the boarding school St. Louis in Amersfoort Holland. When Germany invaded Poland in September 1939 my family escaped from Europe, and I lived briefly in Singapore at my grandmother's home.

This was followed by two years in the United States attending the St. John Marist Brothers School on 76th street in New York.

I returned with my parents in February 1942 from New York to Batavia, but I escaped when the Japanese invaded Java, to live with Mum in Perth. There I completed my schooling at St. Louis in Claremont, a school that has since been merged with "Loreto" to become John the XXIII.

Unfortunately I have no recollection of any school classmates prior to Perth, where my best friend was John Sampson. John became the school athletics champion, and in our last year we were appointed joint officers of the school cadet force.

Despite not belonging anywhere, there have been compensations. Exposed to differing countries and fluency, now lost, in Dutch and Malay, I became familiar with a range of cultures and also food ranging from Asian curries and the delicious flesh of the orange Ramboetan fruit, to Dutch "Poppertjes" pancakes.

Finally, I had twelve settled, peaceful years in Perth to complete my schooling and university degree in civil engineering.

My closest friend at university was Ian Morison who came from Doodlakine in Western Australia and I enjoyed visits to his family farm. In the third year of our degree Ian and I shared six months together in Tasmania working for the Hydro Electric Commission. We rowed together with some success in a pair, four and eight at the University of WA Boat Club.

Later Ian went to the University of London to study town planning while I attended Oxford, and Ian was Best Man at our wedding in London in June 1956. On returning to Australia Ian lived in Canberra and became the city's town planner. We subsequently shared several Christmas holidays with Ian, his wife Pat and their two children at Pambula Beach south of Sydney.

Our closest friend was Frank Costigan whom with wife Kate, we met when our respective children were attending Manreesa kindergarten behind the Immaculate Conception church in Hawthorn. Frank later divorced from Kate, and died in 2009 as a result of a brain tumour.

He collapsed in his Collins street flat on returning from yet another overseas trip, but was able to reach his mobile phone to call his eldest daughter, Phillipa. We still miss him on Saturday mornings when he would come to Domain road to share his favourite Croque Monsieur prepared by Margaret and we would discuss the week's political, legal and social gossip.

Frank was an exceptional man, highly intelligent and with great integrity. He was private and careful not to betray emotion but enjoyed friendships and recognition.

His greatest interest was politics and also overseas travel, fine hotels, books and cars. Unfortunately his marriage broke down as Kate also had strong views and interests. Margaret and I attempted but were unsuccessful in healing the breach when we returned from the United States.

In 1988 we enjoyed a trip with Frank and Ruth Jones to Naples, Ravello and Jerusalem, and then with Frank to Istanbul, Izmir and Amman.

Margaret made the following notes of this trip:

When Ben and I arrived in Rome we checked into the Hotel Excelsior, very grand, and we were surprised that we had been upgraded to a suite, with table loaded with fruit, wine, cheese and various biscotti.

We showered, unpacked a little and went for a little 'passegiata', quite fun as it was the first time we had stayed on the Via Veneto. Came back to get ready to go out for dinner, then changed our minds, helped ourselves to the wine, bread and cheese already set up, and passed out about 7pm. We woke early after a good sleep, surprised not to hear any traffic, went walking and came upon a dear little church where we heard mass, said by Irish Franciscans, about six priests and ten people in all. Invited back for coffee but declined.

Next morning we opted for breakfast around the corner, instead of the very expensive hotel one. Then walked to the bus station, stopping on the way at a church, which started life as the Diocletian Baths, built by 45,000 Christians who barring 12,000 died by the time the Baths were built. The remaining 12,000 were then put to death. Learnt later from Ruth that this was the church I was looking for, where in the basement everything is built from the bones of the martyrs, even the light fittings from finger bones. I first saw this when I was 17, on my trip to Italy with Mum and Dad, accompanied by Father Larry Doyle. We next went by bus to St Paul's 'Fiori I Muri'.

I like this church because of its simplicity and past associations, and the portraits of all the Popes on the walls. Afterwards we went to a local trattoria for lunch, and asked for a mezza boteglio di vino, but they produced a whole bottle, saying, you only pay for what you drink, and of course we drank the lot.

Next day we had breakfast at a local bar, this one cheaper still, because it was a stand-up place in the Via Veneto. We then went shopping and I had my haircut. Quite by chance we came across a travel agency and enquired about a plane from Naples to Jerusalem. They confirmed that Frank and Ruth were booked, but not us and there were only three seats left, so we felt pretty lucky.

Our friendship with Frank was very special for us during our early years of retirement. We interrupted a holiday in Sri Lanka with our son Michael's family to attend and speak at his April 2009 funeral service in St Patrick's Cathedral, which was filled with Melbourne's legal profession and his family and many friends.

Since my retirement I have had the opportunity to think more about religion and God, and read widely on the subject, including the Quran which I found endlessly repetitive! These readings were also stimulated by Michael Lynch's wife Adrienne, who lent me the book "Christ before Christianity" by Albert Nolan, a Dominican priest from South Africa.

Nolan had refused world leadership of the Dominican Order in Rome, believing he could be of more use opposing Apartheid.

I learned in Nolan's book that Mary Magdalene is the Patron Saint of the Dominicans!

Recent books I have read include "The first two millennia of Christianity" by D. MacCulloch of Oxford University.

The only drawback of this excellent and stimulating history is its size, as the book is too large to read in bed or take on a plane.

It has led me to see St. Paul as the centre of Christian ideals, and St. Peter as the origin of the Church structure. It cooled me somewhat on the trappings and dogmas of the Catholic Church and religion, and instead I have become more focussed on Christ and God.

Pope Benedict, when announcing his resignation and speaking at his last mass as Pope in 2013 said,

"The more administrative machinery we construct, be it the most modern, the less place there is of the Spirit, the less place there is for the Lord, and the less freedom there is."

Indeed one can speculate that the Church's labyrinthine bureaucracy has been part of the difficulty of dealing adequately with the Church's sex-based scandals.

I was interested to read Voltaire's comments on seeing a magnificent sunrise,

"Oh mighty God I believe. As to monsieur the son and Madame his mother, that is another matter."

When back in Melbourne in 1993, I visited Father Bill Dalton several times at Campion House on Studley Park Road, in a room on the first floor, which accommodates ill Jesuits. Bill had been stricken with a speech difficulty despite an operation on his throat. He was extremely frustrated with this as he loved discussions. We would discuss family, life and religion.

Early in my career I became aware that there were prejudices against Catholics and this had led some of my school colleagues to enter law, medicine or the public service rather than the business world.

I experienced such prejudice only twice. The first time was when ICI Australia appointed me Company Planning

Manager and the staff let me know that I was only the second Catholic to be made a senior manager in the Company, the other being Tom Conroy then General Manager of the Chemicals Division. The second occasion occurred many years later when I was appointed Chair of a Government Committee to review the compensation and conditions of doctors in Victorian hospitals. When my name was put forward to Cabinet for approval, Premier Kennett commented, "Not another bloody Catholic". Though the appointment was approved.

My changed thinking on religion and the Catholic Church paralleled my increasing interest in the wonders and complexity of science, the universe and our own galaxy.

As scientific discovery has advanced, we understand less of the mysteries of creation, whether in subatomic particle quantum physics, the genetic instructions of the double helix or the complexities of the human cell.

And we remain unable to relate the brain's operation to human functions such as memory, reason, imagination and personality development. As stated by British Astronomer Royal Martin Rees,

"That our brains which evolved 200,000 years ago to cope with life on the African Savannah, should become equipped to understand the deepest levels of reality, and it is rather remarkable we get as far as we can. And just as a chimpanzee can't understand quantum theory, it could be that there are aspects of reality, which are beyond the capacity of our brains.

There is something strange and wonderful that the human brain, a three pounds dollop of jelly evolved to control the bodily functions and behaviour of Palaeolithic hominids and which anatomically has probably not changed a great deal since the African exodus, is capable of contemplating the interior of an atom and the vastness of intergalactic space".

Reading 'Einstein's Mistakes' by Hans C. Ohanian was a revelation to me. Einstein himself later admitted his error in postulating his famous formula 'E = mc2', which links energy with mass. Surprisingly the great scientist and outstanding visionary did not excel in mathematics, where he relied instead on his wife, whom incidentally, he treated atrociously.

My life-long interest in aviation was stimulated when as an engineering student at the Aeronautical Research Laboratory in Melbourne I worked on the stress on the wing of the wartime "Mustang" fighter plane.

This was followed later by my research at Oxford on the stalling problem of a de Haviland aircraft wing. I also tried to join the Oxford University Air Squadron hoping I would thereby learn to fly while at Oxford.

Unfortunately I failed the medical entrance examination and learned that my eyes were weak in "resolving power", although I was told this handicap would be waived in wartime!

I have throughout my life continued this interest in the evolution of commercial and military aircraft.

I mentioned earlier my first flight as a child in 1941 in an un-pressurised DC 4 travelling across the United States. While rowing intervarsity as a student in Perth, I flew in TAA and Ansett-ANA Vickers Viscounts and 'Convairs'.

Later in 1969 I flew in the then largest plane in the world, the Boeing 707, and later the first commercial jets, the French 'Caravelle' and the De Havilland 'Comet', before the latter was grounded following its crash off the coast of Italy killing all on board. When the fuselage was recovered from the seabed it became evident that the disaster was initiated by a stress fracture of the aluminium main wing spar, as a result of wing fluctuations experienced during air turbulence. This metal stress failure was similar therefore to my earlier work on the "Mustang" wing at the ARC in Melbourne.

Margaret and I retraced aviation history, when with Jan and Anna we flew from Hawaii to San Francisco in a propeller driven Boeing 'Stratocruiser', as part of our 1969 journey from Melbourne to ICI in Scotland.

The plane had a second lower deck with a horseshoe seat facing a bar, where passengers could share a drink while the main cabin was transformed to full length sleeping bunks on either side of the aisle.

The plane was comfortable but slow and noisy, with its four powerful propeller driven engines. My favourite propeller driven aircraft was the Lockheed 'Constellation' with its beautifully curved organic shaped fuselage and three pronged tail. I travelled on this plane on two trips to Europe with my ICIANZ boss Ted Kayser in the late 1950s.

More recently Margaret and I have experienced the evolution of the Boeing 747 jet. Initially designed as a cargo plane, which included a small upper pod on the front of the fuselage for the flight crew, the pod was later extended to become a first class passenger cabin with a small lounge and bar at the rear. In later designs this upper area was utilised for sleeping berths and more recently for business class seats on the latest stretched version of the Jumbo. It has been quite an evolution over the years in aircraft size, speed and comfort, but unfortunately offset by increasing delays at airport terminals and deteriorating in-flight service.

The one remarkable technical development in this progression in passenger flying was the super-sonic Concorde. This joint venture of the French and British Governments with its delta wing flew at twice the speed of sound and thus faster than the rotation of the earth. This meant you would see the sun rise in the West after sunset when flying from London to New York.

The cabin was narrow with two seats on either site of the aisle. One felt a slight jolt to your back when the after-burners were turned on to break through the sound barrier, but the plane then became soundless as it left the sound of the engines behind in its wake. At supersonic speed the friction of the thin air would heat the fuselage lengthening the plane by ten inches! This meant the passenger windows had to be small, as larger ones would fall out!

The Concorde flew at 60,000 feet and at that altitude the sky is dark blue and one can actually see the curvature of the earth.

The Concorde started flying commercially in 1976, and I was on its 10th anniversary flight from London to New York in 1986.

The British Airways (BA) Chairman and other dignitaries together with entertainers and a band were in the BA Lounge to see us off. The departure celebration was followed unfortunately by the plane having to return to the terminal an hour later having suffered an engine fault, when we were greeted by cleaners sweeping up confetti and party debris!

I flew Concorde repeatedly across the Atlantic to attend

and report to Monday morning ICI Board meetings in London. This was during the year when ICI purchased Beatrice Chemicals, and I was temporarily its chief executive and based in Boston.

It became routine for me to leave Wilmington on the ICI Americas' Falcon jet on a Saturday morning and fly to the BA terminal at JFK in New York. As I would enter the terminal lounge from the Company "Falcon" parked on the nearby tarmac, for the three and a half hour flight to London.

On one occasion, BA had a promotion offering a free return flight for a partner. Margaret of course was keen to accompany me for a day's shopping in London. However the plan went awry, as when after my ICI meeting I returned to the ICI Americas flat in Arlington Street off Piccadilly (near the Ritz Hotel), to collect Margaret for the return to New York, I found her asleep. She awoke disappointed that she had missed her day's shopping!

The development of aircraft, initially made of wood and canvas, then aluminium and recently incorporating carbon fibre reinforced plastic composites, is likely to continue to be subsonic as the Concorde took its last flight in 1993 following a disastrous fire on take-off in Paris.

Further technical advances are likely to be made primarily by the military, though exceptions to this generalisation are the recent radical aircraft design developments by MIT and the Imperial College London[22].

A major current aim of this work is to improve airflow over wings to maximise laminar flow, as turbulence creates

22 Economist 12/3/11

drag. About half the fuel required to maintain a plane's level flight, is burned to overcome drag resulting from the turbulent boundary layer on the wings. This was a key aspect of my research at Oxford when I studied the transition from laminar flow to turbulent air on a wing in a wind tunnel there.

I have been fortunate in my business career in experiencing major changes in technology. Such as commercial explosives, which had been based on gunpowder or 'black powder' until replaced in the 1900s by nitro-glycerine as a result of Alfred Nobel's discovery.

My early career as an engineer witnessed the last days of black powder manufacture at Deer Park. But when in Glasgow designing a new nitro-glycerine (NG) plant utilising Swedish technology for a new plant to be built at Bass Point in NSW, the project was stillborn as NG was being replaced by Ammonium Nitrate/Fuel Oil.

The latter is the simple fertiliser based explosive, now favoured by terrorists.

Another significant change in technology followed the early development of plastics. Machinery was developed to extrude, mould or blow the new plastic materials. This resulted in widely used products such as shopping bags, bottles, pipe and film.

When I arrived at Plastics Division headquarters in 1973, the largest building on the site housed such equipment used to educate and familiarise customers in the use of plastics but by the end of the decade the building was full of obsolete unused machinery. And the use of plastics for photographic film was made obsolete by digital electronic cameras.

The instant camera "Polaroid", a major ICI customer of ICI's Plastics Division in the 1970's, no longer exists.

I touched on the accelerating change in technology during my lifetime in the speech I gave at a Melbourne University graduation ceremony in 2007.[23]

ICI struggled when it attempted to change from a commodity focussed company by acquiring the specialty chemicals business of the Beatrice Company in the United States in 1985 and had little understanding of customers needing downstream products such as adhesives, shampoos and hair conditioners.

The Beatrice group of seven separate businesses was an eye-opener with its specialty 'Stahl' leather finishes, 'Converters' printing inks, 'Thoro' building sealants, and 'Imperial' oils and greases. The one downstream exception acquired from Beatrice was 'Fiberite', which manufactured carbon fibre for the USAF stealth fighter and bomber as well as the exhaust nozzles for the NASA Space Shuttle.

There were of course a few established ICI speciality products such as 'Dulux' paint supplying consumers.

Following the retirement of ICI Plc's Managing Director Ronnie Hampel in London, the Company appointed as replacement Charles Miller-Smith, who had recently missed being appointed the chief executive of Unilever. He proved to be a failure finding it too difficult to change ICI's embedded culture.

In our ICI and holiday travels we visited a range of countries and cities, some of great interest such as Izmir (formerly Smyrna in Turkey) where with Frank we gambled at a casino

---

23 Address at University of Melbourne Conferring of Degrees. p277

after visiting Ephesus, the place where the Virgin Mary is said to have died, after being taken there by the evangelist John.

But ICI work usually impeded my ability to enjoy local culture and colour.

Thus visits to Teheran in 1990 before the Shah was overthrown, and Beirut before recent wars when it was the Monaco of the East, had to be cursory and spent mostly in offices and hotels.

This also applied to my Russian and Chinese visits, when my only excursions were limited to the Catholic Cathedral in Canton, and the Bolshoi Ballet and a deserted Orthodox Cathedral in Moscow.

Returning to recent interests and readings about life and the world about us, why as humans are we here?

The French Quaker missionary Stephen Grellet, who lived from 1773 to 1855 put it well when he stated, "I expect to pass this world but once; any good things therefore that I can do, or any kindness that I can show to any fellow creature, let me do it now: let me not defer or neglect it, for I shall not pass this way again."

I have in no way satisfied Grellet's dictum, but Margaret and I have achieved a wonderful legacy in our seven children.

But I need to qualify this immediately and admit that a major part of the credit for the development of our children as wonderful individuals is due to Margaret.

I inevitably played a minor role in their day-to-day upbringing as I was away so much of the time, but I like to think that together, we showed them that it is possible to have a loving relationship in a marriage that has lasted 60 years.

We have attempted to influence them to be sensitive to others and be concerned about those less fortunate than ourselves.

They are all wonderful people and we are blessed and very proud of them and our grandchildren.

In recent years Margaret and I have been able to share family get-togethers or trips away with our children. In 1997 Margaret took our daughters Anna, Maggie and Lucy to Italy, and stayed in an apartment overlooking the Grand Canal in Venice.

That same year I took our sons Jan, Mark, Michael and Benedict on a trip to Hawaii for some golf and deep sea fishing. Ten years later our sons organised a trip for us to attend the Rugby World Cup in Wales and Scotland.

In December 2003, we rented three adjoining beach properties in Belongil Beach near Byron Bay, for a week with the whole family including grandchildren and more recently, the family celebrated together for a week in 2010 at 'Carmel by the Sea' in Broadbeach Queensland.

They have all been times with special memories.

A major initiative stimulated by Margaret on retirement was our interest in the plight of refugee children in detention camps.

This support reached a peak following the 'Tampa' crisis in 2001, when Prime Minister John Howard placed Australian troops aboard this Norwegian vessel, which had saved refugees from a boat which sank near Christmas Island. This occurred just before the Federal election in 2004.

Press Advertisement. 2004.

As a result of meeting Julian Burnside, a high profile Melbourne lawyer and very active supporter of refugees, we placed advertisements in the Melbourne and Sydney papers. The ads included a child's drawing of refugee children behind barbed wire and drew considerable media and public attention.

We also have supported the Brigidene Sisters who continue to be very active in helping refugees. One Afghan refugee we met through the Sisters was Phillip Aliniazare.

We tried to offer him casual work cleaning our back courtyard and helping with drinks at one of our yearly volunteers "thank-you" evenings for the Parish homeless project, but he refused payment.

We were surprised later when the front door bell rang by none other than Phillip, who wanted to introduce us to a buxom girl standing beside him named Irene who was his Greek fiancée. We were honoured to later be invited to their Greek Orthodox wedding and reception in Brunswick.

Margaret on our return to Australia also resumed her interest in Italian. She enrolled in language courses in Carlton, and followed this with two visits to a language school in Sienna, the second accompanied by our daughter, Maggie.

In 2002 Margaret and I went to Italy for three months so that Margaret could attend art courses in Pienza, Lucca, Otranto in Puglia and Bologna. We also stayed one week with an Italian family in Viterbo, arranged by the Dante Aligieri Society. While Margaret attended her lessons I sketched or painted local scenes, and would join her for lunch.

Margaret and my interest in painting included two trips we made with a group led by painter Margaret Cowling, the first to Sicily and the Aolian Islands and the second in country Victoria. Our painting interest, now in watercolours, continues to this day as we attend weekly classes with Pat Winnett at the Camberwell Community Centre. I have become fascinated, perhaps through painting, in the beauty of nature particularly in the ever-changing clouds and colour of the sky.

A further reflection is that I was indeed fortunate that my father never having completed secondary school insisted that Jesuits educate me. As a result when I arrived in Australia in 1942, I attended St. Louis, generously on a no-fee basis. Later I graduated from the University of Western Australia, which at the time was free. And as a Rhodes Scholar I was able to complete my post-graduate degree supported financially. So apart from a few primary school years, my education was free.

This is in sharp contrast to the burden our children have experienced educating our grandchildren. I have benefitted greatly from my broad education, and as stated by the Indian poet, writer and educator Tagore (1861-1941),

"The main object of education is to knock on the doors of the mind".

It has been Margaret's and my good fortune that we were able to educate our children. We were helped with school fees when, in England, ICI bore this cost as a condition of my secondment from Australia.

It leads me to reflect on how one's financial circumstances are influenced by unforeseen events.

Thus since my retirement from ICI Americas, my pension halved initially as the US dollar declined in value opposite the Australian dollar partly a result of US Government economic mismanagement.

And earlier in my life, although my father had sought to provide for my mother with his large personal insurance policy, this became worthless as a result of Indonesia becoming independent after his death. So much for attempts to secure one's financial security in this rapidly changing world.

19

My Father's Death in 1945

Jan Lochtenberg's grave.
Located in Bandung, Jakarta

Dad died in a Japanese POW camp in Pekanbaru, a town in Central Sumatra.

After the capture of Singapore, the Japanese wanted rail access to mine coal near Pekanbaru and also to provide an alternative route from Singapore to Sumatra's west coast. The Japanese Military used POWs to build the railway from Padang on the west coast to the coal deposits in the central mountains of the island. A number of successive camps were built, as construction of the railway progressed.

According to Hank Hovinga's book 'Eindstation Pekanbaru', work started soon after the first prisoners of war arrived at Camp 1 on 19th May 1944 having left Batavia's port, Tandjong Priok, in Java on Sunday May 14th.

A month later on June 26th 1944, another ship, the "Van Waerwijck" laden with POW's also destined for Pekanbaru, was torpedoed near Bengkulu on Sumatra's west coast.

Several other ships transported POW's to work on the railway, and on September 18th 1944 the Junyo Maru was also torpedoed off the west coast of Sumatra.

Hovinga's book states that about 2000 Dutch and some English and Australian POWs worked on the railway.

The "Far East POW" Forum held in March 1976 provides the following additional information about "The Other Railway" in Sumatra:

Under the Netherlands administration, a railway had existed from PADANG on the west coast of Sumatra to a railhead at Moeara, about 80km to the northeast as the crow flies.

The line itself was much longer as it wound through the mountain ranges. It seems that there was a fair quality of black coal to be had in this area among other produce. Towards the northeast across the eastern mountain slopes and the flatter terrain along the east coast lay the up river port of Pekanbaru.

From here, down the Siak River, a regular shipping service plied to Singapore. A plan to build an extension of the railway between Moeara and Pekanbaru had been devised back in 1920 to provide a connection between Padang and Singapore faster than the long sea routes around the north or south tips of the island. A better quality of coal existed in the area between the two points so that such a railway would benefit the transport of the mines output.

Now, whereas the Nippon plan to revive the Burma - Thailand link obviously had some strategic value to their attack on India, it is not clear why they literally dug up the Sumatra project.

With all oil available from Borneo and South Sumatra, it would seem that the coal was not the answer. However, militarily, it could have provided better facilities for troop movement in the event of expected Allied attack on West Sumatra as early as 1944. Logistical support from Singapore and the mainland would have only a short sea passage to the up river port, thus lessening the danger of Allied submarine attention, which at that time, was making a great nuisance of itself to the Greater Asia Co-Prosperity Cause.

So on May 25th 1944 work started on the line from the Pekanbaru end. The line headed roughly southward and slightly west as it neared the Equator with large bridges across the Kampar Right and Kampar Left Rivers.

Many of the POWs had been brought from Java by sea up the west coast to the port for Padang at Emmerhaven. Thence by rail to a point from whence a motor road led across the island to Pekanbaru. Others came from Singapore and Medan up the Siak River in an old ferry boat, the 'Elizabeth', known as the White Ship.

Some 1,450 POWs were lost at sea by submarine action

on the west coast route and a further 176 were lost similarly between Medan and Pekanbaru.

A total of 6,593 POWs were used in addition to native labour. Included were a number of Norwegian seamen who had been torpedoed by a German submarine in the area. Some 513 POWs died on the line. Rails and locomotives were sent from the east coast of Sumatra at Medan; also Java and Malaya.

My father's involvement in this railway, similar to the infamous Thailand-Burmese railway which my Uncle Harold worked on, was told me by my Uncle Joop who survived the War in Java and returned via Sydney to Holland with his wife Corrie and their three boys, and also by a Pekanbaru POW survivor, Mr Serks, whom I met on the ship when I travelled from Melbourne to Oxford in 1954.

According to Uncle Joop and Mr Serks, Dad along with many other Java-based POWs, were taken on a Japanese merchant ship to Sumatra. Japanese sea movement of POW's was common during the war, usually involving transport to work in factories in Japan, as happened to my Uncle Bevis La Cloche, who was shipped as a prisoner from Changi to Japan. Conditions on these POW ships are captured by Frank Foster in "Comrades in Bondage":

In dead silence we were ushered below into the murky holds which had been converted into shelves about four feet from ceiling to floor. It just gave you sitting room, with no room to stand up or stretch your legs which were aching after the march (to Tandjong Priok).

*In the bowls of this ship we could see nothing but a small
patch of blue sky through the hatch.
When the new year dawned,
We were duly warned-
We were destined for a trip
And we left Java isle,
Without song or a smile
On a Nippon prison ship.*

*So we left the port,
Which was our fort-
When we landed a year before
And though we fought,
We were badly caught,
And now sailing for Singapore.*

*Away down in the hold,
Amid cobwebs and mould-
We were herded together like sheep;
On a choppy sea, We drank saltwater tea,
And rice which would make you weep."
"Comrades in Bondage" by Frank Foster, Skeffington,*[24]

My father's ship was sunk by a submarine near Sumatra. I have not learned whether he was on the 'Van Waerwijk', torpedoed off the coast of Sumatra on the 26th June 1944, or was on the 'Junyo Maru", which I learned of when visiting the Australian War Memorial in Canberra in May 2005.

The book, "Prisoners of the Japanese in World War 2 by Van Waterford, makes no mention of the sinking of the 'Van Waerwijk', but only the 'Junyo Maru' which sailed from

---

24 'Skeffington', Frank Foster. 1946. p 67 & 68

Batavia on September 15th or 16th, and was torpedoed on September 18th west of Benkulen west Sumatra by the British submarine HMS Tradewind.

On board this later ship were 2200 POW's including 1700 Dutch, British and Australians, and 4320 Javanese conscript labourers known as Marushas. 1520 of the former died and 4120 of the latter, making it the least reported but largest maritime disaster in world history.

Van Waterford speculates that this disinterest is because two-thirds of the victims were Indonesians natives.

According to the survivor Mr Serks, the submarine to its surprise after the sinking, saw a sea full of survivors obviously too numerous to be the sunken ship's crew. The submarine then surfaced and at great danger to itself remained on the surface to ferry groups of POWs to the nearby coast of Sumatra, at which point POWs would jump into the sea to swim ashore. The submarine performed this operation repeatedly saving many POWs, hoping not to be sighted by a Japanese plane or ship.

But once ashore, the POWs were only to be recaptured by the Japanese, and one can imagine the hardships endured by my father whether he was among the one-third survivors from the 'Junyo Maru' or the 'Van Waerwijck'. All of this preceded the later trials he would endure when building the Pekanbaru railway.

Throughout the war, Mum and I never received any letters or news of Dad. It was not until well after the War ended in August 1945, that we finally received advice on November 14th from the Red Cross of my father's death.

The news arrived in the post as a small piece of lavatory

paper with a short message that my father had died at Pekanbaru in Sumatra on May 6th 1945 because of several tropical diseases and malnutrition.

Dad's Death Notice in Dutch received later from the Pekanbaru Camp Doctor, also via the Red Cross, had the following further details:

The deceased Mr Lochtenberg has therefore had a chronic inflammation of the intestine, much diarrhea, probably as a consequence of dysentery. These ailments have worn him out in a high degree (marasmus) added to this he acquired beri-beri from which he finally died.

Generally speaking these patients are very calm and die quickly.

The burial place of kamp 2 is now very nicely cared for. On each grave (there are more than 400!) a wooden cross and a wooden monument for the whole graveyard with the inscription: Ego sum resurrectio et vita.

Berri-berri is a crippling disease caused by vitamin B deficiency, affecting muscles, heart, nerves and the digestive system. The Singhalese-based word translates as "I can't, I can't". The other affliction caused by vitamin B1 deficiency was "happy feet", a gnawing, burning sensation in the soles of the feet which would force men to hobble up and down at night seeking relief from their discomfort.

Mum had lived in hope throughout the war despite the lack of information about Dad. She collapsed when she received the brutally short message of his death.

It led to severe depression and prolonged personal suffering. Her immediate reaction was to give or sell any possessions with past associations of Dad, such as her rings and some mementos such as silver objects and the ivory mah-jong set. She sought comfort increasingly in sleeping tablets to escape reality.

Unfortunately Mum was not strong enough mentally to face a future without Dad and as a result she focussed her sole interest on me. Her misery amplified by her brother Harold and the husbands of her sisters, Nan and Alice having survived the war.

What had, for me, previously had been a loving and self-sacrificing mother became a somewhat demanding and mentally damaged person. I attempted to understand her suffering and confront the changed situation as best I could. My aunt, Nan and grandmother, Anna were particularly supportive to me at that time.

The extreme hardship Dad endured as a POW are described in COFEPOW South East Asia, under Japanese Occupation. "The Sumatra Death Railway", available online[25]:

Pakanbaru to Muara

They ate starch and rats, they died of exhaustion dysentery and tropical sores, but on 15 August 1945, the last year of the war, and the day that the red Japanese sun finally went down, the death railway from Pekanbaru to Muara was ready. The last nail that the scarred survivors drove into the last sleeper in the Sumatran jungle was one of copper for lack of a gold one.

The railway line built by Dutch, English and Australian

---

25 http://www.cofepow.org.uk/pages/asia_sumatra3.html

prisoners of war and by press-ganged Javanese slave labour (Romushas) through marshy forest of central Sumatra under orders from Japanese occupiers had taken a toll in human lives of nearly 700 whites and of probably more than 10,000 people altogether.

And this does not include the 1,626 victims who perished on the way to Sumatra, torpedoed by the Allies on board the 'Van Waerwijck' and 'Junyo Maru'. No one will ever know the exact number of dead press-ganged Romushas. It is certain that the remains of thousands of these browned skinned slaves lie under the sleepers of a railway line, which was never to see a train after 1945. All the suffering in this case was for nothing.
The railway line no longer exists. Kilometers of rail have been looted or sold as scrap iron. And what remains is slowly rusting away in the stagnant black marsh water of the impenetrable Sumatran Jungle.

When the Japanese capitulated on 15 August 1945, officially confirmed on the 2nd September, the curtain fell on the tragedy of Pekanbaru. Even in Asia the end had come at last to the most horrific war of all time. Historians were able to weigh events up, survivors to tell or record their bitter war experiences, and filmmakers got in on the act with their romanticised account of the 'Bridge Over the River Kwai' on the famous and much-

described Burma railway. All the events of those terrible war years in the Far East were researched and written up in documents and books.
Almost all, for due to some mysterious reason are not

solved even today, there has never been an account of the gigantic drama of the 215km death railway from Pekanbaru to Muara in the heart of tropical Sumatra, with its snakes, panthers, tigers and billions of malaria carrying mosquitoes.

The suffering, the power of the Japanese and Korean guards and the fruitless death of so many simply remains engraved on the hearts of the survivors.
A few still keep the notices and announcements published just after their liberation. But they are never publicised. The drama of Pakanbaru is forgotten.
Even in Indonesia.

Even in today's Pakanbaru, where children happily play on the remains of locomotives and trucks, without themselves realising at all that the rusty playthings between their campong huts are the last silent witnesses to a nightmare of suffering which was also real.

Maggots on the menu

For most of the POW's, who were brought from Singapore or Padang, entering Camp 1, fittingly named 'Mud Fun', at the edge of the Bakan Baru campong, was often their introduction to the railway.
From there they were sent to other camps along the line to cut sleepers from wood, build bridges over the rivers, and to fix rails on the track. But for anyone becoming seriously ill and unable to work, the final destination was camp 2 - the death camp on the Pekanbaru line, where few doctors fought using primitive equipment a generally hopeless campaign against death. One of

these was military surgeon W.J. van Ramshorst from The Hague, who operated and amputated with a few simple knives and bent forks as "sharp hooks", when the tropical sores of his patients had eaten through to the bones.

Dr. van Ramshorst remembers:
"We had no medicines and no antibiotics if someone had to lose a leg, the amputation made you feel a bit faint. I did have a bottle of ether, but when I had to operate on an acute ulcer one evening, in the crazy hut of bamboo poles and palm leaves.

I could not use my petroleum burner for fear of explosions. Camp mates from the work shift stole a battery from a Japanese truck, and by the one slim ray of light from this battery I was able to help my patient. Those who did not work, i.e. the sick, were on half rations, mere 800 calories a day.
The dying got nothing at all, as no-one passed them anything. But this was hardly noticed amid all the other suffering. As a result we very soon had a hundred dead per month. The inmates of Camp 2 consisted of approximately 800 men. So I told a Jap, "Another 8 months and everyone will be dead".
He replied: "Splendid, that's precisely the idea".
Nevertheless we got through it.

It was worst at night, the rats ran all over you, but once caught in a homemade trap of spring and a small board, they made a tasty meal. They had marvellous white flesh, even whiter than rabbit pieces. I saw chickens grubbing round the latrines and quickly getting fat from the maggots. And I thought: what's good for chickens is good for people too. So we fetched maggots by the bucketful out of the latrines, washed them, cooked them and gave them with sambal (sauce) to the sick, which then visibly improved because of this extra portion of protein. And in fact I made another discovery in that terrible camp, where people only actually came from the railway to die. We had no disinfectant for treating dirty tropical sores, but once again the maggots provided a solution. I wound an old sheet with maggots in it round a wound and after a few days it was nicely healed.

Only peeled rice was issued, without the vitamin rich silver skins, so many died of malnutrition, beri-berri, malaria and bacillary dysentery, for which there was hardly any cure. But we were able to save a number of people with the maggots. When the surrender came at last we got a double portion of rice.

All of a sudden we were allowed out of camp. I walked to a post office Pekanbaru and asked the crazy question whether I could send a telegram to my wife in Java. And, strange as it may seem, I was able to for 10 cents per word. The Japanese were extremely jumpy and when they had burnt all papers relating to the camp they asked us if we thought that they should commit suicide. Our answer was: "Yes, as your tradition hara kirri lays down, that's the best thing you could do".
In the bridge building camp we had to pile drive trees into the river.

The Japs were very careful over the tools given out. From time to time a monkey wrench would crash down into the river, and if we found it we would be given tobacco and extra food. So more and more monkey wrenches started to fall into the water, but we had tied them to a stick beforehand with very thin thread. The first train was pushed over the bridge by 150 POWs. We never thought it would take it, for the whole thing was mainly clamped together. The train got to the other side but the bridge was distorted by the very first river flood. And then there were the tigers. The place was stiff with them. Ever since a Japanese had gone to sit on the latrine one night and had been eaten by a tiger, they were scared to death of them.

Now, there was a certain Jan de Kwant in our gang, who could do a marvelous imitation of a tiger. When Jan gave a growl in the evenings, the Japs fled inside and we were able to quietly steal a chicken from the guards camp, which Jan plucked under his mosquito net, trembling the from fever because he had again caught malaria.

A bridge had to erected across a wide river and our gang had to chop trees from marsh forest. When we did not jump from the path into the water ourselves, we were beaten into it. We stood shoulder deep in the water and sometimes our heads went under. The amazing thing is that nobody was eaten by crocodiles. The worst part was when a tree finally fell. You had to try and get out of the way, while a torrent of red ants rained down on you.

After one to three weeks the bridge was ready and then the rain came. The river swept trees and bushes out of the jungle and we POWs had to work at night, trying to steer driftwood between the bridge piles using long sticks. But the next day there was no denying that the bridge had a bend in it. No one believed that a train would ever get over it, but the Japanese knew better.

Then, when we all had to get in the very first train, I thought my last hour had come. But with a lot of whistling and creaking we made it to the other side.
Because the wretched railway was easily disrupted and the clamped bridges just held together, there were many derailments. Sometimes we had to use brute force to get trucks back on the track. I still do not know how we managed to right a heavy locomotive and get it back in place. We had to raise it using loose bits of rail and push it centimetre by centimetre. It didn't work at first, obviously, but when the swine gave the signal "Lift" and at the same moment began to beat us at random, we finally succeeded. Everything succeeded in this way by the end.

Between Logas and Muara we dug our way through a hill carrying away the earth in baskets. And we laid a railway line in a narrow ravine under an overhanging mountain from which bits kept falling off. When the first trainload of Romushas went along this line, the cliff fell in and they were all buried alive.

The exhausted POWs who were forced during the Japanese occupation to construct a railway line 215 km

*long right through mid-Sumatran tropical jungle had
no escape. For over a year, from late May 1944 until
Japanese capitulation on 15 August 1945, they were
subject to the whims of their cruel Korean guards and
to their Japanese masters, who had been ordered by
Tokyo to construct a railway line between Pekanbaru
and Muara at the cost of so many human lives. They
acquitted themselves very well in this task. More than
10,000 native slave labourers and nearly 700 whites,
mostly Dutch POWs died in the torrid Sumatran jungle
of malnutrition, beri-beri, tropical sores, malaria and
dysentery."*

The number of Romushas, or native labour, who worked
on the railway, was estimated by H. Neumann in the
"Sumatra Railway" in 1984, to be the much higher figure
of 30,000 of whom about 80% died.

POW deaths totalled 706 of whom 499 were Dutch.
Neumann also describes POW food rations in the camps.

Japanese treatment of all POWs, such as Dad, was
influenced by the "martial and harsh discipline of
"Bushido", a moral military code developed in Japan in
the early 12th century for Samurai warriors. It has seven
essential doctrines,

The first is righteousness, which comprises justice and duty.
The second is moral rather than physical courage, deeply
rooted in honour. The third is humanity, attributed specifically
to the ruling class. The fourth is respect, not only to authority
and elders, but also to all others. The fifth is sincerity, the sixth
honour and the seventh is loyalty.

The code encouraged soldiers to accept "duty is weightier

than a mountain, while death is lighter than a feather."[26] and it has been said that "The Japanese soldier would rather die in battle than live with the shame of surrender and, as the Allied defenders of Malaya, Singapore and the Phillipines discovered, he despised those who didn't share that view."[27]

At the end of the war, 482,000 Japanese soldiers surrendered in South East Asia, and a year later 116,313 were still to be repatriated and many of them had disappeared rather than return to Japan.

The POW camps for the Pekanbaru railway were administered by the 25th Japanese Army headquartered in Singapore. Until March 1943 the commander was Lieutenant General Saito Yaheita who was succeeded by Lieutenant General Tanabe Moritake. After the war both were sentenced to death and executed for their treatment and torture of the Pekanbaru POWs. The local commander of railway construction was Captain Miyasaki Ryohei who was also sentenced to death on May 31st 1948 for carrying out his orders inhumanely.

The camp guards were Japanese soldiers but also conscripted Koreans. Many of the Pekanbaru guards were imprisoned after the war for five to twenty years in Sigamo prison in Tokyo. Japanese military men were brought to trial at the Tribunal set up by General Douglas MacArthur as a demonstration of "victor's justice".

There were critics even among the Tribunal's judges who believed if a trial of war criminals was to be "just", it had to proceed without double standards.

---

26 Prof. Adachi of Japan's National Defence Academy – "Hellfire" by Cameron Forbes. 2005. p 34 & 35

27 'Kill the Tiger' Peter Thompson and Robert Macklin, Hodder 2002. p 31

The Allies had ordered saturation firebombing of civilians in scores of cities such as Hamburg and Tokyo, and atomic bombing of Hiroshima and Nagasaki. On 9th March 1945, 334 B29 bombers of the United States Air Force dropped 500,000 petroleum bombs on the wooden and bamboo houses of Tokyo causing a firestorm which claimed 80,000 lives and made one million homeless. Sixteen square miles of the city were destroyed.

The raid occurred two months before Dad's death in May. The "Little Boy" atomic bomb was dropped on Hiroshima on August 6th, and following no response from the Japanese Government, a second bomb named "Fat Man" was dropped on Nagasaki on August 9th, leading to the cease-fire by the Japanese on August 15th 1945, and the signing of surrender on the ship "Missouri" in Tokyo harbour on September 2nd.

The two bombs that initiated temperatures equal to the centre of the sun and horrific long-term radiation affects, as well as immediate deaths of 40,000 and 75,000 respectively at the two cities. The Tribunal ruled against implicating these bombings by the Allies.

Dad's death after three years of captivity, was ironically on VE Day May 8th 1945, which marked the end of the War in Europe. A further bitter twist to his captivity and trials at Pekanbaru was that the railway was completed on the 15th August 1945, the day hostilities ended in the war with Japan. The railway therefore was never used by the Japanese, as intended, and according to later war historians, the long three months delay between the war's end and the advice Mum and I received about his death was a direct result of the Allies bypassing the Dutch East Indies in their final onslaught on Japan. This was influenced partly by the United States policy at that time, to end Dutch and other European colonialism in the Far East.

I have often reflected on Dad's life with its periods of hardship, such as during late childhood in World War 1 and later when unemployed during the Depression.

These were interspersed with the excitement of his early years when he went to South East Asia, and his later success culminating in two years of virtual business independence when he was based in New York. But this came to an abrupt end when he endured extreme suffering before dying in the jungles of Sumatra as a Japanese prisoner of war at the young age of 42.

20

My Mother

I have found it personally difficult to write about Mum whom I knew as "Deen". She was a loving, devoted mother, but a very unhappy and disturbed person from the time of my father's death. Mum grew up in Singapore with five sisters who married expatriate Europeans (Bernard Murcott and Bevis La Cloche), or white colonials (Joe Atkins and Henry Drennan), and the youngest sister later married a Swiss (Irwin Meyer). So when Dad joined the family household as a boarder it is not surprising that it was not long before Mum in 1930 married this Dutchman who had been working in Java.

But in less than a year after their wedding the worldwide Depression occurred resulting in Dad losing his job, and Mum's initial married happiness was dashed. The couple, with me a newborn baby, decided to leave Singapore and seek employment in Holland.

It was Mum's mother, Anna Rosa, who paid the fares for the voyage to Europe. In Amsterdam, the family lived with Dad's parents and this was a very stressful time for

Mum. Her situation aggravated by Dad's continuing failure to obtain employment, and in contrast to the married and settled life of her sisters in Singapore.

Dad no doubt influenced by Mum, decided after a year to return to the Far East. Happier years for the family then followed in Java, culminating when my parents went to Europe on long service leave in the summer of 1939.

This was also when they placed me in a boarding school in Amersfoort, Holland. The trip to Holland must have been very satisfying for my father, returning to Amsterdam with his family. But the short and happy interlude ended with the outbreak of war in September.

Mum then became separated from Dad, as she and I escaped by ship to Singapore to live again with my grandmother, whereas Dad was sent by his German company to open an office in the United States, to buy US sourced steel products for shipment to Java.

So from the time of her wedding, Mum's life had its ups and downs until the final separation from Dad when Mum and I escaped from Java to Australia in 1942. From that time, aged 38, she battled on alone bringing me up, working initially as a bookkeeper in a small engineering repair business near our home and employed later in the accounts department at the University of Western Australia. But she suffered periods of depression from the time she learned of Dad's death as a POW and she also became increasingly possessive and her focus on me continued for the rest of her life. Although she never had shown interest in my girlfriends in Perth, she appeared to welcome my early mention of Margaret, being a daughter of the senior surgeon at the Brisbane Mater hospital.

However, this early acceptance changed when Margaret and I became engaged, particularly when Margaret moved in 1954 from Brisbane to Perth, to work as a nurse at the Hollywood Repatriation hospital. Mum realised that Margaret would be taking away her son and only child, who had become the centre of her life.

Unfortunately she was unable to accept Margaret, nor hide her feelings. Typically when Margaret arrived from the hospital before a meal time, Mum would say,

"You have eaten haven't you?"

with the result that Margaret would watch us eat although hungry herself. Mum continued to betray her feelings in later years, making comments such as, "Your marriage is all give and take, Ben gives and you take".

My engagement to Margaret and leaving Perth in 1954 to take up a scholarship at Oxford increased Mum's loneliness and self-absorption.

Unhappily she did not have the strength and acceptance to deal with this new situation, despite earlier pleasure in my success. She remained unhappy and depressed when we returned from England in 1957 and also when she moved from Perth to live with us in Jocelyn Court Melbourne.

Our small dining room, which adjoined the kitchen, became her bedroom. However, this arrangement became an increasing problem in our small two-bedroom home and with our growing family of three small children.

This led to Margaret buying Mum a flat in Elgin Avenue in Armadale when she received a bequest from her mother's estate. However Mum was never happy with her new home which was in Margaret's name, believing that should I die,

Margaret would sell the property and make her homeless.

Mum's unhappiness was influenced by her opposition to Margaret who was stronger and more secure.

Throughout the years before her death Mum would suffer repetitive bouts of deep depression and regularly over medicate herself. On one occasion she narrowly avoided setting fire to her nightgown when we found her collapsed next to a radiant floor heater.

It finally became necessary to hospitalise Mum in Larundel, a psychiatric Melbourne institution now closed.

At another time we were able to admit her for two months in a Ballarat hospice where she was cared for by nuns and where we would visit her on weekends. Mum's life became a succession of crises interspersed with periods of relative calm. During the latter she would sit contentedly in her Armadale flat, knitting clothing for her grandchildren whom she loved, or the Red Cross as well as school and church fetes.

Mum never took any exercise and smoked incessantly, but enjoyed her coffee and an occasional glass of sherry in the evening. She read little other than magazines, but was a good writer and kept in touch with her sisters in Perth and two brothers in Sydney. Her lonely life continued during the twenty years we were moved successively by ICI to England and then the United States and Canada, although the original intention was for us to be overseas for only three years.

Our long absence was interrupted only by our yearly visits to Australia, or when she would join us when we lived in the United States.

However crises continued in these later years, as when she telephoned from Melbourne to say she had been raped and was in hospital. My immediate reaction was to fly to Australia, but Margaret suggested we should first check her situation, so we rang a doctor and friend, Brian McKay in Melbourne, and asked him to check on my mother's condition. He confirmed that Mum was not in any Melbourne hospital but remained at her flat in Armadale. He explained that it was not uncommon for elderly women to make such a claim. This was a cry for attention and wanting me to demonstrate my love for her.

Many of these episodes have faded from memory but it was an unhappy time, especially for Mum, and of course affected our family. Although I understood why she never accepted Margaret, it is unfortunate that she was unable to do so. It remains the only conflict and difficulty I have experienced in my life.

My ICI move to England by ICI in 1973 did result in some acceptance and calm for Mum. When we were based later in the United States for fourteen years from 1979, she would visit and stay with us each year at Chadds Ford.

She also during these years, developed a close relationship with a nearby Armadale nursing home, into which she would check herself whenever she felt a need. We learned later that she maintained this good relationship by paying for maintenance replacements at the nursing home, and buying a car for the owner/manager.

Unhappily she died suddenly with no warning, alone in her bedroom from a ruptured aorta on the 4th June 1987, before we were able to come to Melbourne.

All we were able to accomplish when we arrived was arrange her funeral service, at which our Jesuit friend Father

Bill Dalton officiated, burying her in Springvale Cemetery. We disposed of her few possessions and arranged for the sale of her apartment in Elgin Avenue, before we returned to the United States. What was personally very distressing was to dispose of Mum's blood-stained mattress.

Mum's life contrasted starkly with my own, which has not been affected by loneliness but blessed with family and friends in a life of comfort and relative affluence.

Fortune can play cruel tricks as it did to my mother and father. However I also remember my father's happier times, which were generally full of optimism and goodwill. My childhood was very secure and happy, and I believed my Father and Mother loved one another, and that both were proud and delighted with their only child.

However I learned much later from my Aunt Nan that when we were living in New York, Dad was keen to have another child and according to Nan he was extremely upset when he learned that Mum had taken steps to avoid becoming pregnant again. Should this be true, it must have been a strained time in their marriage.

A postscript to my father's life was when Margaret and I together with my cousin 'Big Ben' and his wife Charlotte visited his grave in Java in April 1986.

I had written to the Dutch War Graves Commission in The Hague seeking information about Dad's grave, and learned that all Dutch POWs who had died throughout Indonesia had been transferred after the war to eleven official Dutch War Cemeteries in Java.

Dad's remains were moved to a cemetery called 'Pandu', in Bandung south of Djakarta. We visited his War Cemetery grave after meeting 'Big Ben' and Charlotte in Singapore at the original Raffles Hotel, which then still had its open-air breakfast courtyard filled with plants and caged brightly coloured tropical birds, and austere basic bedrooms off this courtyard. Though that colonial setting has since been replaced by the up-market luxury new Raffles Hotel.

From Singapore we flew to Medan in Northern Sumatra, and then driven in a hair-raising two day journey through narrow roads crowded with oxen, chickens, cyclists and teeming people, to Lake Toba and its island of Samur. The island is the original cone in the centre of a fifty by fifteen mile lake inside the old primeval volcano, which according to geologists erupted some 70,000 years ago.

The super volcano at what is now Lake Toba in Sumatra, erupted with a strength more than 1000 times that of Mount St Helens in 1980, throwing some 800 cubic kilometres of ash into the skies. It is believed the eruption is the largest in the last 25 million years. The ash lowered global temperatures and pushed world climate to the edge of an ice age. Some scientists speculate that the earth went into a deep-freeze, and that most humans then alive were killed and the population of Homo Sapiens may have dropped as low as a few thousand families. Some believe that the catastrophe created a human "bottleneck" in Central Eastern Africa and India affecting the genetic inheritance of all humans today.

Samur Island is now a blissful oasis inhabited not by Indonesian Muslims, but settled centuries ago by Buddhists from North Vietnam/Thailand. The women work in the rice 'sawahs' with their children strapped to their backs, while their menfolk play cards under thatch-covered shelters between the paddy fields. It was a restful interlude for the four of us before seeking Dad's grave.

After Sumatra we flew from Medan to Djakarta and then by road to Bandung, a mountain resort in Central Java south of Djakarta. I had great difficulty getting a taxi driver to take us to Dad's cemetery because of Malay fear of 'Mabok' or ghosts. However we were able finally to bribe a driver to take us to the Pandu address given me by the War Graves Commission.

When we reached Pandu we argued with the driver that he had mistakenly taken us to a wrong location, but he insisted the address was correct.

We were concerned that we were not at a war memorial, as we appeared to be at an old colonial cemetery overtaken by jungle vines and which had fallen into disuse and decay. We stumbled through this old cemetery and found a door in a back wall covered in greenery. To our surprise we entered an immaculately kept walled cemetery, which contained nearly 4,000 white crosses in neat rows.

I had been given Dad's grave number and an old Indonesian attendant directed us to Dad's grave, with a cross showing his death as "5-5-45". However all the official notifications as well as the message we received from Camp 2 where he died, state May 6th 1945.

It was an extremely emotional visit bringing memories of my father and the sufferings and privation he endured.

It was very comforting to share this visit with Margaret, Charlotte and Big Ben. But it was upsetting to observe the dates on all those graves, as most crosses had 1945, with very few in 1943 or 1944.

My father and the others just could not survive three or more years of harsh Japanese captivity.

Dad's final resting place near Bandung is by chance near the quinine plantation where previously he had worked on his first job as a young man.

After this very emotional visit, we went to a Javanese resort on the south coast, hopefully to recover at a reportedly luxury hotel which in fact was run down and almost derelict, with an empty outdoor pool and broken reclining chairs. However, a nearby fishing village made the trip interesting, with its large covered fish market and fishing boats.

The remnants of colonialism were still alive in this remote part of Indonesia no longer frequented by tourists. As we walked back along the coast road from the village to our hotel, a passing small bus stopped for us. The driver forced a couple of Indonesian passengers to get off as the bus was overcrowded, so as to make room for us. We were very appreciative, although we felt sorry for those evicted when we realised this had happened on our behalf.

We next flew with Big Ben and Charlotte to Bali, but on our arrival Big Ben received word that his mother Corrie was dying, so they left the next day. Unfortunately they were unable to reach Holland before she died. It was a sad ending to an eventful trip full of painful memories.

We moved hotels the day Big Ben and Charlotte left as Margaret was startled by a snake lying at the entrance to our Balinese bungalow. We moved to the Oberoi Hotel and completed our Indonesian visit in comfort, but reflective of our time in Indonesia

PETA JALAN KERETA API
MUARO/SIJUNJUNG-PEKANBARU
220 KM

Sumber: De Pekanbaroe Spoorweg

Kamp No 1

Sungai Siak

PEKANBARU

Kamp No 2
Tangkerang

Kamp No 3
Kubang km 15

Tugu Peringatan
Kerja Simpang Tiga

Danau Bingkuang

Teratak buluh

S. Kampar Kanan

Bangkinang

Kamp No 4
km 19

Kamp No 5
km 23 Lubuk Sekat Juli 1944

Kamp 6 km 35
Sungai Pagar
Oktober 1944

Kebun Durian

Sungai Pagar

Lipat Kain
km 75

Kamp 7
Desember 1944

Kamp 7A km 69
22 April 1944

S. Kampar Kiri

Limbanang

Tanjung Bauh

Kamp No 8 km 111
Kotabaru Mei 1945

Payakumbuh

Peta

Sungai Bawang
Km no 9

Km 142 Logas

Logas

Kamp 14
Taput 3
1 November 1944

Loge Tanko

ke Lubu Sikaping

S. Sabangan

Jalan
Kerata Api

Bukit tinggi

Muara Lembu

ke Rengat

Padang Panjang

S. Ombilin

Kamp 12 km 200
12 Juli 1945

Km 11
km 176

Teluk Kuantan

S. Indragiri

Durian Gadang
Silokat

S. Kuantan

Km no 10
km 160

SUMATERA HINDIA

Batang Anai

Kamp 13
Muaro, 7 Maret 1945

Lubuk Ambacang

Muara Kalaban

Sijok

Lubuk Jambi

PADANG

MUARO SIJUNJUNG

Tambang Batu Bara
Ombilin Sawah Lunto

Tempat pertemuah pembangunan
Jalan Kereta Api dua arah

ke Jambi

ke Painan

★ Barak-barak tawanan perang
- - - - - Jalan kereta api

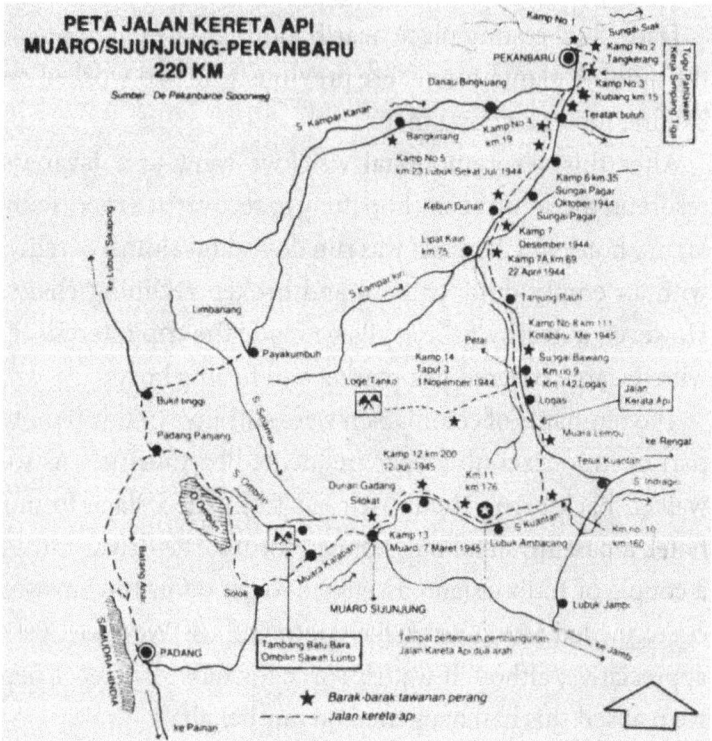

1944 Map Detailing Camp Locations and the Proposed Railway

266

21

The Lochtenbergs

Unfortunately I know very little about the history of the Lochtenberg family except for my father's parents who lived in Amsterdam. I met them in 1938 when my parents and I visited Holland.

My Dutch grandparents, Bernardus Johannes Marie (whose parents were Hermanus Johannus L., 1844 – 1905, and Alida Albertina Wessels, 1846 – 1906), and Maria Dorothea (daughter of Arie Ruhe ,1848 – 1927), were born in 1872 and 1875 respectfully. They had a large family of four daughters and nine sons with Dad being the third son and fourth child, born on the 25th November 1902.

They were a strict and disciplined Catholic household, and Dad throughout his life remained a regular churchgoer and was adamant that I attend Catholic, and if at all possible, Jesuit schools.

Lochtenberg in the 1940s was an unusual if not unique Dutch name and I was told that the family name would have died out with my grandfather Bernardus, except that he had nine sons and seven of them also had sons ensuring continuation of the Lochtenberg family name.

Joop, Dad's elder brother told me an intriguing, but to date unconfirmed, story about the origin of the family name Lochtenberg. This story passed down to Joop, was of a Scottish mercenary of the "Lochlen" clan (my spelling but there are many possible variants: Lachlan, Laughlan, McLoughlin, etc.). This possible forbear came to Holland to fight with the army of William of Orange in the wars against the Spanish, later settling in Holland with his name at some point altering to Lochtenberg, perhaps through marriage. Was Lochtenberg a corruption of "Lochlen" thus referring to the Scottish origin, by adding "berg", which is Dutch for "mountain", or possibly recalling the topography of Scotland?

The story piqued my interest and raises many unanswered questions. In late 2002 I came across Henry Kamen's book "Spain's Road to Empire" published that year, confirming the use of Scottish mercenaries in the Dutch wars against Spain. This book also examines the strong link between Spain and the Netherlands in the 16th Century during the reign of the Spanish king Phillip II.

Spain and the Netherlands had enjoyed a close relationship after the late middle Ages. Spaniards were generally unfamiliar with the countries of Northern Europe, with which they traded little, and whose language and culture remained a mystery to them. The one exception to this was the Netherlands, with which they traded directly by sea and which in turn imparted its financial expertise and cultural creativity to the Iberian Peninsula[28].

---

28 'Spain's Road to Empire', Henry Kamen p 77

And from the early 16th century, the Netherlands was directly under Spanish control becoming a province of the Spanish branch of the Hapsburgs.

Phillip II's father Ferdinand had already enlisted mercenaries during 1487 to 1491, from Switzerland, France, Italy, Germany and England.

These soldiers together with those from Castile, drove the Moors out of Granada[29]. Scots are not mentioned by Kamen in this Spanish campaign, and the possibility of a "Lochlen" then being involved is remote. More likely are the Wars between Spain and the Netherlands, which came about as a result of the Reformation. This led to a strengthening in the Netherlands of heresy laws including the death penalty, and imposition of new taxes.

"The Dutch aristocracy revolted in 1566 by resigning their offices, and a group of lower nobility led by Prince William of Orange demanded religious freedom and the suppression of the Netherlands Inquisition".[30]

Phillip II sent the Duke of Alba to Holland to suppress the insurrection. It was unprecedented to send an army into a friendly province in a time of peace. Alba carried out arrests, confiscations and executions, regardless of religion whether Calvinist or Catholic. This was followed by sackings and massacres in several Dutch cities. The city garrison of 2000 Dutchmen in Haarlem "were executed in cold blood in 1572"[31] and in the same year the Huguenot leader Admiral Coligny was murdered (an interesting

---

29 ibid p 16

30 ibid p 177

31 ibid p 187

historical link with the fleeing to Germany of Mum's Huguenot ancestors the Godeffroys).

The Dutch/Spanish Wars did not end until 1576, when peace was negotiated in Ghent. This required the withdrawal of Spanish troops and the acceptance of religious freedom in the seven most Northerly districts, including Holland, Zeeland and Friesland.

After 1576, a stalemate developed between the Netherlands Republic in the North and the Spanish controlled Catholic Flanders and Brabant in the South, the two areas separated by the Waal and Maas rivers.

Behind this river barrier,

"Holland and Zeeland enjoyed absolute immunity after 1576, and mercenaries were garrisoned in the frontier towns or lay in camps and manoeuvred on the other side of the rivers." [32] "The sea was a great factor in this development, and opened the country to wealth and power." [33]

"Wealthy Holland was beginning to attract mercenaries and adventurers from all sides" [34]

The sudden rush of "colonial enterprises began about this time as the Netherlands people escaped from the stifling embrace of the Spanish Monarchy with its bureaucratic and aristocratic regime. The whole of Holland and Zealand was humming with activity. [35]

One can speculate reasonably that the Scottish mercenary "Lochlen" was active in these Dutch Wars during 1566 to

---

32 'The Revolt of the Netherlands 1555-1609' Pieter Geyl.1988

33 ibid p 234

34 ibid p 235

35 ibid p 233

1576, under the command of William of Orange, resulting in his settlement in Holland. Alternatively he may have served during the less arduous last quarter of the sixteenth century.

A further possibility is that he served later in the Dutch army commanded by Maurice of Nassau in the Wars against Spain from 1610 to 1621. This "Dutch" army, "included not only Dutchmen, but French, German, Belgian, Frisian, English and Scottish soldiers" [36]

In 1648 under the Treaty of Westphalia, Spain recognised the independence of what was then called the Republic of the Netherlands, headed by members of the Orange-Nassau family as 'Stadhouders' or Governors. The Netherlands became the monarchy it is today only in 1815. The area now Belgium, split away in 1830.

It is perhaps appropriate to end this attempt to record my family background and journey in these scattered threads of history relating to the Lochtenbergs. And I have become increasingly aware that there is also an equally interesting story to be told of my wife Margaret and her Lynch/O'Hara Irish family origins.

36   ibid p 164 and p 320

Proposal for Award of Honorary
Degree of Doctor of Laws

Dr Bernard Hendrik Lochtenberg
BEng *WA* DPhil *Oxf* FTSE

Born in 1931 in Singapore, Dr Bernard Lochtenberg settled in Australia in 1942. He was educated at the University of Western Australia, graduating with a Bachelor of Engineering (Honours) degree, and, as a Rhodes Scholar, at the University of Oxford, graduating with a Doctor of Philosophy degree.

Dr Lochtenberg joined ICI Australia in 1956. He became a Manager of the company 1970, and a director in 1973. He was a senior Vice-President of ICI Americas from 1979 to 1988, and Chairman from 1989 to 1993.

Dr Lochtenberg was Chairman of Orica Limited, formerly ICI Australia, from 1995 to 2001.

Dr Lochtenberg has been a most active and capable contributor in a wide range of health organisations. In 1994-1995 he was a Director of the Caritas Christi Hospice (Kew) and has been Chairman of the Mental Health Research Institute since 1994 and a Director of the Inner and Eastern Health Care Network Board since 1995.

He was a member of the Neuroscience Victoria Board from 2002 to 2004. Dr Lochtenberg was also Chairman of the Ministerial Review on Medical Staffing in the Victorian Public Hospital System in 1994-1995.

Dr Lochtenberg has made an outstanding contribution to the University in his role as a member of University Council. Dr Lochtenberg was appointed a member of the University Council 1996 and was subsequently appointed as Deputy Chancellor in 2005. He has been an active member of Council committees, namely Audit and Risk Committee (1998-2004), Building and Estates Committee (1998-2006), Remuneration and Employment Conditions Committee (formerly Standing Committee on Staff Salaries) (1996-2006), Council Nominations and Governance Committee (2004-2006), Senior Appointments Committee (2005) and Honours Committee (2006). He has also been a member of the Newman College Council since 1996.

To cite a long list of committee work and university subsidiaries can seem worthy but perhaps not exciting. Yet it is through these various bodies that Council members exercise leadership within the University.

In his long involvement on Council, Dr Lochtenberg has contributed to almost every significant facet of the institution. His influence has been subtle, continuous, and highly valued.

In 1998 Dr Lochtenberg undertook the important leadership role in the establishment and governance of UMEE Pty Ltd (formerly Melbourne University Private Pty Ltd) by first accepting a directorship of the company, which was then followed by his appointment as Chairman in 2003.

In 2001, he also took on the role of Director of Melbourne Enterprises International Ltd, a subsidiary of UMEE Pty Ltd, which was followed by his appointment as Chair in

2003. In 2004, he took up the appointment of Chair of the MU Student Union Ltd, which he held until May 2006.

Dr Lochtenberg has also been Chairman of the Delaware Symphony 1984 – 1993.

In 2003, the Commonwealth Government awarded him a Federation Centenary Medal, acknowledging his great contribution to the Australian community.

Address at University of Melbourne Conferring of Degrees
21 March 2007

"It is a great honour the University has done me today which I will always remember.

It has been a privilege for me to be associated with some wonderful people at this great university, with its totally committed staff and colleagues on Council. Thank you for the honour. It is one of life's paradoxes that when you enjoy something very much, you are also rewarded as I have been.

Now to come to the important part of what I want to briefly say this evening, namely those of you who have been awarded degrees. All of you are now ready after your hard work and sacrifice, to gain from what life in future has in store for you. In looking at you, I echo what another ageing man the Renaissance Dutch Scholar Erasmus exclaimed 500 years ago:

"Oh to be young again!"

How does a 76 year old communicate here tonight with a diverse group full of energy, vitality and promise? You are the future movers and shakers, and potential leaders in your various areas of interest, both here and in so many other countries.

Perhaps I can comment on my own experiences to indicate to you that life brings many opportunities and changes in direction that you must grasp.

Some of the changes I have experienced may possibly confront you in the years ahead. This is particularly likely since knowledge, technology and society are continuing to accelerate their change. This is of course illustrated in this university as it embarks through the leadership of Chancellor Ian Renard and Vice Chancellor Glyn Davis on the course and curriculum changes of "Growing Esteem" beginning next year.

To return to my own history, I was born in 1931 of Dutch parents in Singapore where some here tonight originate. 1931 was a time of world depression and therefore not an auspicious time to be born. It was also the year Al Capone went to jail in Chicago. And when I was two in 1933, an Austrian soldier named Hitler became Chancellor of Germany, and coincidentally a movie appeared called "King Kong", about a large destructive ape!

My early schooling was at a boarding school in Holland near the German border. However I was fortunate to escape from the European war as my father took me out of school the day Hitler invaded Poland in September 1939. This marked the end of a blissful pre-war era, and a film appeared that year appropriately named "Gone with the Wind" starring Vivien Leigh and Clark Gable.

It was also the year the first commercial TV appeared in the United States. And more ominously, although no one was aware of the implications at the time, a scientist named Dr Otto Hahn in Berlin's Kaiser Wilhelm Institute bombarded a bit of uranium with neutrons and for the first time split the atom.

I lived the next two years in New York, but the family was not to escape war as I accompanied my parents on a visit to Indonesia when the Japanese attacked Pearl Harbour in December 1941. Everyone needs some luck and I guess I was the beneficiary of that in February 1942 when I escaped from Batavia, now Djakarta, on a cattle boat with my mother together with 500 other refugees.

We left in a convoy of ships heading for India. But for some reason, our boat left the convoy and headed for Australia. We learned later that many of the ships heading for India were sunk, so I was indeed fortunate to have survived and to have come here. However my father's luck ran out as he was unable to leave Java and died later in a prisoner of war camp.

After arriving in Perth I completed my schooling there, followed by an engineering degree at the University of Western Australia. My later post graduate work in Oxford was on a wind tunnel where I was able to study a problem of a new plane designed by de Havilland, now British Aerospace. A subsequent offer of employment by this British company was trumped by ICI Australia who offered me an engineering job in Melbourne. So this turned out to be another sharp turn in my career, as I wanted to return to Australia. Although I only planned to be with the company for a few years, I remained with the ICI Group until my retirement in 1993, with more than half of my working career in England and the United States.

I tell you all this as your own career may well have some twists and turns as mine did. 1956 when I left Oxford was a time of change in many ways including entertainment. A gyrating singer named Elvis Presley became a star overnight, and Marilyn Monroe made an impact on impressionable minds such as mine in a movie named "Bus Stop".

Jumping ahead, 1969 saw me for three months at Stanford University in California. Students were even more active then having been stirred up by the Vietnam War. They even burned down the University President's office while I was there, which perhaps held me in good stead when I was asked to become involved in the Student Union here! It was also the year that 400,000 attended an event called Woodstock on the East coast, and pop-rock was the new craze with a musical called "Hair".

It was a year of scientific milestones. Neil Armstrong was the first man to walk on the moon. The microprocessor became a chip. Genetic engineering saw the first photo of a gene, and as a counter to this scientific explosion, Mother Theresa started her work in Calcutta.

With so many changes and events in my life, I marvel at what will become commonplace to you, and the exciting scientific and social opportunities that face you in the years ahead. I urge you to grasp these future opportunities.

Most of my working life from 1973 to 1993 was initially in England but mostly in the United States and Canada. 1973 was the first year of the traumatic Watergate crisis, which led to the impeachment of President Richard Nixon. And a movie in 1973 was appropriately named "The Godfather".

The Vietnam peace agreement was signed that year and the Boeing 747 flew for the first time.

What are my impressions of Australia since returning in 1993 One major impression relates to a topic which continues to receive much publicity here, relating to refugees and mixed cultures. No doubt I am interested in this having been an early refugee myself. I became aware after my return how much Australia has changed in its ethnic and multicultural mix. We are indeed fortunate in how far we have come. I urge you to continue along this path, and to learn from and respect the views of others, particularly minorities.

You have your new degrees tonight and I congratulate you on your achievement and wish you every success in future. As I indicated earlier, what a tremendous time in these years of a new century to grasp the many opportunities ahead, as you launch your vocation and career.

I wish you and your family good fortune.
Thank you."

Ben and Margaret now enjoy retirement in their
Melbourne home, and continue their interest in refugees,
the homeless and painting classes. They spend time
whenever possible with their children and grandchildren

They will celebrate their 60th Wedding Anniversary
in June 2016

A Boy on the Last Boat

Ben Lochtenberg

ISBN:	9781925367416	Qty:	.....
	RRP	AU	$26.99
Postage within Australia		AU	$5.00
	TOTAL★	$_____	

★ All prices include GST

Name:..

Address: ....

....

Phone:...

Email: ....

Payment: ❑ Money Order ❑ Cheque ❑ MasterCard ❑ Visa

Cardholder's Name:..

Credit Card Number: ....

Signature:...

Expiry Date: ....

Allow 7 days for delivery.

Payment to: Marzocco Consultancy (ABN 14 067 257 390)
                   PO Box 12544
                   A'Beckett Street, Melbourne, 8006
                   Victoria, Australia
                   admin@brolgapublishing.com.au

Be Published

Publish through a successful publisher.
Brolga Publishing is represented through:
• **National** book trade distribution, including sales,
marketing & distribution through **Macmillan Australia.**
• **International** book trade distribution to
    • The United Kingdom
    • North America
    • Sales representation in South East Asia
• **Worldwide e-Book distribution**

For details and inquiries, contact:
Brolga Publishing Pty Ltd
PO Box 12544
A'Beckett St VIC 8006

Phone: 0414 608 494
markzocchi@brolgapublishing.com.au
ABN: 46 063 962 443
(Email for a catalogue request)

www.ingramcontent.com/pod-product-compliance
Lightning Source LLC
Chambersburg PA
CBHW070942100426
42737CB00011BA/1393